Complex PTSD

A Practical Guide to Overcome Traumatic Events and and Live a Peaceful Life

(The Complete Guide to Understanding, Treating and Recovering From Trauma)

George Moore

Published By **Oliver Leish**

George Moore

Complex PTSD: A Practical Guide to Overcome Traumatic Events and and Live a Peaceful Life (The Complete Guide to Understanding, Treating and Recovering From Trauma)

ISBN 978-1-998927-01-2

No part of this guidebook shall be reproduced in any form without permission in writing from the publisher except in the case of brief quotations embodied in critical articles or reviews.

Legal & Disclaimer

The information contained in this book is not designed to replace or take the place of any form of medicine or professional medical advice. The information in this book has been provided for educational & entertainment purposes only.

The information contained in this book has been compiled from sources deemed reliable, and it is accurate to the best of the Author's knowledge; however, the Author cannot guarantee its accuracy and validity and cannot be held liable for any errors or omissions. Changes are periodically made to this book. You must consult your doctor or get professional medical advice before using any of the suggested remedies, techniques, or information in this book.

Table Of Contents

Chapter 1: What To Understand Approximately Ptsd

The definition of put up annoying strain sickness (PTSD)

A intellectual ailment known as posttraumatic strain illness (PTSD) can strike absolutely everyone who have long beyond thru or witnessed a stressful incident like a herbal disaster, a terrible twist of fate, a terrorist assault, struggle, or rape, or who have confronted threats of demise, sexual attack, or excessive damage.

PTSD has been noted with the resource of many unique titles inside the beyond, collectively with "shell surprise" in some unspecified time inside the future of World War I and "battle exhaustion" following World War II, although it does now not simply have an effect on veterans of armed battle. All humans, no matter race, state, or way of lifestyles, can get PTSD at any age. An predicted one in eleven human beings will receive a PTSD diagnosis in their lifetime, and it influences spherical three.Five percent of person U.S. Citizens each yr. PTSD influences women greater frequently than it does adult guys. U.S. Latinos, African Americans, and American Indians are 3 ethnic corporations which can be disproportionately impacted and feature more charges of PTSD than non-Latino whites.

Long after the bad incident has surpassed, PTSD sufferers are plagued via vibrant, unsettling thoughts and sensations relating to their experience. They may additionally experience desires or flashbacks of the incident, experience melancholy, dread, or fury, and revel in remote or estranged from other humans as a result. Persons who have PTSD might also avoid settings or humans that lead them to consider the disturbing experience, and they'll additionally reply negatively to apparently unimportant such things as a noisy noise or an unintentional contact.

An frightening worrying incident must have been professional so you can diagnose PTSD. However, the exposure couldn't be direct but alternatively oblique. When a person learns of the violent passing of a near relative or pal, for instance, PTSD can also additionally moreover set in. Additionally, it could display up at the same time as people are time and again uncovered to unsightly facts of trauma, such whilst cops are exposed to specifics of little one abuse instances.

The symptoms and signs and symptoms and the prognosis

The following 4 commands fantastic describe PTSD signs and symptoms. The depth of a given symptom can also exchange.

Intrusion: Persistent, uncontrollable recollections; frightening nightmares; or flashbacks to the annoying incident. People may additionally undergo flashbacks which are so vivid that accept as actual with they'll be reliving the lousy occasion or are seeing it in the the front in their very eyes.

Avoidance: Avoiding the worrying event's reminders can also entail avoiding human beings, locations, sports activities, items, and situations that might bring once more ugly reminiscences. It's common for humans to want to overlook about or now not think about the painful revel in. They can be reluctant to talk about what took place or their feelings round it.

Changes in cognition and temper encompass the dearth of capacity to consider important facts of the traumatic event, bad emotions that result in continual and distorted beliefs about oneself or others (e.G., "I am awful," "No one can be trusted"), distorted thoughts about what brought on or resulted from the event that result in setting blame on oneself or others, persistent worry, horror, anger, guilt, or shame, a extensive decline in interest in once-cherished sports activities, and a feeling of estrangement (a void of happiness or satisfaction).

Changes to arousal and reactivity: Arousal and reactive symptoms may likely consist of irritability and livid outbursts, reckless or self-negative conduct, being quite privy to one's surroundings in a suspicious manner, being quick startled, having hassle focusing or snoozing, as well as being overly alert of one's surroundings.

In the times that have a look at a worrying occurrence, many people who had been exposed to it stumble upon signs and symptoms paying homage to those stated above. However, symptoms and symptoms of PTSD have to persist for introduced than a month and offer a intense ache or purposeful task for the affected individual so as for a evaluation to be made. Many people have symptoms and signs and signs and symptoms three months after the incident, notwithstanding the fact that signs and symptoms can occasionally rise up later and may final for weeks, months, or possibly years. Depression, substance abuse, memory issues, similarly to different problems with physical and intellectual fitness, are often gift along PTSD.

Additional Conditions

Disorder of acute pressure

Like PTSD, acute strain disorder additionally outcomes from traumatic activities, and every problems have comparable signs and symptoms. However, the symptoms and symptoms and signs display up three days to a month after the incident. Acute stress sickness patients also can relive the event, experience flashbacks or dreams, and sense numb or disconnected from themselves. Significant pain and issues are brought on through those signs of their each day lives. Acute stress disorder is observed through PTSD in about 1/2 of sufferers.

Acute stress ailment is notion to have an impact on between 20 and 50 percent of sufferers of attack, rape, or mass shootings, and between thirteen and 21 percent of vehicle twist of destiny survivors.

In order to control signs and signs and symptoms and symptoms and prevent them from developing worse and turning into PTSD, psychotherapy, specifically cognitive conduct treatment, is beneficial. SSRI antidepressants are one elegance of medicine that might assist with the signs and symptoms.

Disorder of Adjustment

In response to a annoying life enjoy, adjustment infection develops (or sports). The emotional or behavioral signs and symptoms that someone feels because of the stressor are often extra acute or immoderate than what may be anticipated under the sports.

Feeling annoying, depressed, or despairing; withdrawing from others; appearing defiantly or swiftly; or physical manifestations like tremors, palpitations, and headaches are only some examples of signs and signs. The symptoms and symptoms can seriously impair a person's capability to carry out in key spheres in their life, which consist of at manner, college, or in social situations.

Adjustment contamination signs and symptoms and signs and symptoms appear three months after a stressful incident and disappear no greater than six months after the stressor or its effects have passed.

A unmarried stressor, this kind of breakdown in a love dating, can also moreover arise, or there may be numerous stressors that have an additive impact. Stressors can be persistent or continual (together with an ongoing painful contamination with developing disability). Individuals, families, and larger organizations or agencies may additionally additionally all be impacted with the resource of stressors (for example, within the case of a natural catastrophe).

Adjustment illness is the primary analysis of amongst five% and 20% of sufferers receiving outpatient intellectual health care. According to a present day study, adjustment infection affected extra than 15% of parents with maximum cancers. Psychotherapy is often used as treatment.

Social Engagement Disorder with Disinhibition

Children who've gone thru large social forget about approximately or deprivation in advance than the age of are more likely to expand disinhibited social engagement contamination. Similar to reactive attachment sickness, it can increase whilst kids lack the basic emotional necessities for romance, exhilaration, and luxury, or even as not unusual adjustments in caregivers (such common foster care changes) prevent children from developing solid bonds.

A teenager with disinhibited social engagement sickness engages in excessively familiar or culturally beside the factor behavior with strangers who're adults. The teenager need to, for instance, have little to no reservations approximately going out with a weird individual. The infant's ability to connect with adults and classmates is hampered through technique of those actions. The signs and symptoms come to be better whilst the youngster is placed in a everyday disturbing placing. Even after being positioned in a supportive placing, some kids' signs and symptoms ultimate until puberty. The ailment may also co-exist with developmental abnormalities, particularly linguistic and cognitive deficits.

Disinhibited social engagement disorder is doubtful in terms of occurrence however is concept to be uncommon. Most kids who've been disregarded badly in no way accumulate the scenario. During treatment, the child and circle of relatives paintings collectively with a therapist to decorate their connection.

Disrupted attachment response

Children with big social overlook about or deprivation finally of infancy are more likely to increase reactive attachment ailment. It can take location while children lack the easy emotional necessities for affection, pleasure, and luxury, or on the same time as time and again changing caregivers (such frequently switching foster homes) prevent youngsters from developing enduring relationships.

Reactive attachment illness makes children emotionally a ways off from the adults who're being involved for them. They do no longer often are seeking the help, comfort, or safety of carers or show no sign of suffering at the equal time as comforted. They show off minimal remarkable feeling and probably normal dread or grief within the direction of regular encounters with caretakers. The issues begin earlier than age five. Delays in improvement, especially those in language and cognition, often coexist with the infection.

Even with seriously mistreated children, reactive attachment sickness is uncommon. During remedy, the kid and family art work together with a therapist to improve their connection.

Treatment

It is critical to recognize that not all and sundry who suffers trauma goes immediately to acquire PTSD, and no longer absolutely everyone who does now not require psychiatric care. Some people's PTSD signs depart surely over time. With the aid of their guide community, others get higher (own family, friends or clergy). However, many human beings with PTSD require expert care that allows you to get over their intellectual struggling, which may be excessive and incapacitating. It's important to maintain in thoughts that trauma can reason really distressing signs and symptoms. The ache is not the person's fault, and PTSD may be treated. The likelihood of recuperation is higher the sooner someone receives treatment.

Psychiatrists and unique mental health specialists make use of severa green (research-hooked up) strategies to useful useful resource patients in their recovery from PTSD. Effective evidence-primarily based definitely treatments for PTSD consist of each speak treatment (psychotherapy) and remedy.

Behavioral Cognitive Therapy

Cognitive behavior remedies (CBT) are one shape of psychotherapy that is mainly a achievement. Among the CBT techniques used to treat PTSD are cognitive processing treatment, lengthy-time period publicity remedy, and pressure inoculation treatment (positive under).

The aim of cognitive processing treatment is to alternate uncomfortable terrible emotions and mind added on with the useful resource of the trauma, together with "I clearly have failed" and "the arena is volatile." The man or woman is assisted through the use of therapists in going via such provoking reminiscences and feelings.

In order to help someone face and overcome anxiety and ache and discover ways to manipulate, prolonged publicity remedy employs incremental exposures to symptom "triggers" or repetitive, specific imaginings of the trauma. In order to assist PTSD patients relive the battlefield in a regular and recuperation manner, digital fact systems had been hired.

Similar to how a vaccine is run to save you contamination after publicity to a sickness, the intention of strain immunization remedy is to provide the patient with the essential coping mechanisms to effectively guard towards disturbing events.

In a stable and judgment-unfastened environment, institution remedy permits sufferers of comparable disturbing conditions to talk about their feelings and research. Group individuals useful resource every other in knowing that many incredible people may have reacted and felt the identical way. Because the PTSD victim's behavior and agony can impact the complete circle of relatives, circle of relatives counseling will also be beneficial.

Interpersonal, supportive, and psychodynamic remedies, among others, deliver attention to the emotional and interpersonal factors of PTSD. People who do not need to be spherical reminders in their traumas can also locate them useful.

Medication

The symptoms of PTSD may be controlled with remedy. Additionally, medicinal drug's capacity to reduce symptoms and signs allows many sufferers to interact in psychotherapy greater productively.

SSRIs and SNRIs (selective serotonin re-uptake inhibitors and serotonin-norepinephrine re-uptake inhibitors), kinds of antidepressants, are frequently used to treat the number one signs and symptoms and signs of PTSD. Both by myself and together with extraordinary treatment plans collectively with psychotherapy, they are employed.

Other capsules may be used to cope with the nightmares and sleep issues that plague many PTSD sufferers, similarly to to lessen tension and bodily ache.

Different Therapies

Additional healing techniques, including complementary and opportunity remedies, are being more and more hired to resource human beings with PTSD. These strategies offer care outside of the same old intellectual health facility and could consist of an awful lot less talking and disclosure than psychotherapy. Examples encompass animal-assisted remedy and acupuncture.

Many PTSD patients discover that talking to others who have experienced comparable subjects, such in a peer help enterprise, may be quite beneficial further to remedy.

What triggers PTSD?

The fight-or-flight response is the traumatic device's reaction to a traumatic scenario. Your blood strain will growth, your coronary coronary heart price quickens, and your muscle agencies annoying up, presenting you with greater power and quicker reactions. Your frightened system soothes your body as quickly as a risk has exceeded, bringing your blood strain and pulse price again to everyday.

When a condition stresses you out excessively, PTSD develops. Although the risk has exceeded, your worried machine remains "caught," making it hard for it to move again to its normal country of stability and maintaining you from getting over the incident. In order to heal and get beyond the trauma, PTSD recuperation includes aiding your worried device in being "unstuck."

PTSD versus an normal response to terrible activities

The signs and symptoms and symptoms of PTSD are felt with the aid of really anybody to a point after experiencing a annoying occasion this kind of natural catastrophe, twist of destiny, terrorist assault, or assault. It's not unusual to have unbalanced, indifferent, or numb emotions on the same time as your revel in of safety and agree with are violated. It's pretty regular to experience nightmares, enjoy terror, and find out it hard to vicinity the occasions at the back of you. These are not unusual responses to unusual sports.

However, those signs are frequently quick for maximum humans. Although they may final for masses days or perhaps weeks, they in the end disappear. However, when you have positioned up-annoying pressure illness, the signs and symptoms and signs and symptoms and signs do not get higher with time and also you don't experience worse every day. In truth, you may begin to experience worse.

PTSD signs and signs

Because everybody has a in particular top notch neural device and stress tolerance, PTSD develops in a notable way in every person. It might likely once in a while take weeks, months, or even years for PTSD symptoms and symptoms and signs and symptoms to expose up, in spite of the reality that they'll be maximum likely to accomplish that inside the hours or days that examine a disturbing experience. Symptoms might probable sometimes seem to boom out of nowhere. Other instances, they'll be brought on through things like sounds, attractions, terms, smells, or pics that conjure up the initial demanding experience.

Although anyone with PTSD has a totally specific revel in, there are four huge commands of signs.

the annoying incident being relieved thru bothersome memories, flashbacks, nightmares, or sturdy emotional or bodily reactions while the trauma is added up.

Avoidance and numbing, which incorporates warding off topics that make you consider you studied of the trauma, dropping the capability to bear in thoughts positive data of the revel in, losing interest in sports and lifestyles in preferred, feeling emotionally numb and emotionally reduce off from others, and having a restricted outlook on the future.

The symptoms and signs of hyperarousal include trouble falling or staying asleep, impatience, hypervigilance (constantly "on pink alert"), feeling jittery or with out difficulty startled, furious outbursts, and violent, reckless, or self-poor behavior.

wondering styles and mood swings which can be terrible, which include feeling by myself and alienated, having trouble focusing or remembering, being depressed and despairing, feeling betrayed and mistrusted, and feeling responsible, ashamed, or answerable for one's personal actions.

Children with PTSD signs and symptoms

PTSD symptoms and signs in kids, particularly very younger youngsters, might be special from the ones in adults and can include:

Anxiety of being eliminated from their mother and father.

a loss of formerly obtained competencies (together with relaxation room education).

nightmares and troubles with sleep.

gloomy, obsessive drama that capabilities recurring motifs or trauma-related data.

new fears and concerns that do not seem to be connected to the trauma (alongside aspect fear of monsters).

playacting, storytelling, or innovative representations of the enjoy.

Aches and pains that do not seem to have a motive.

Aggression and irritability

You might also additionally have PTSD.

You want to appearance a professional mental fitness professional in case you respond "certain" to three or greater of the subsequent questions because you may have PTSD.

Have you visible or long beyond thru a terrifying, probably deadly event?

Did you feel completely terrified, aggravating, or powerless after this revel in?

Are you having issues forgetting the incident?

Do you balk more with out a problem and enjoy angrier or extra angry than you probably did earlier than the incident?

Do you make an effort to influence clear of situations, people, or thoughts that convey the incident to mind?

Do you discover it harder to concentrate now than you possibly did earlier than the incident to doze off?

Have you had those symptoms and signs and symptoms for longer than a month?

Can you parent or feature well regardless of your misery?

PTSD danger signs and symptoms and symptoms

There are severa danger elements that increase your sensitivity, even though it's difficult to count on who may also revel in PTSD because of stress. The nature of the stressful incident itself has a number one function in numerous chance variables. When your lifestyles or non-public protection is considerably threatened at some stage in a worrying incident, you are more likely to expand PTSD as a reaction. The more acute and continual the danger, the higher the danger. Additionally, intentional, human-prompted damage—collectively with rape, assault, and torture—regularly has a greater mental effect than "acts of God" or certainly one of a kind, greater impersonal mishaps and screw ups. It additionally subjects to what diploma the worrying incident became unavoidable, out of control, and inevitable.

Additional PTSD chance factors are as follows:

preceding annoying activities, mainly those that befell early in life.

PTSD or depression runs in the own family.

abuse records, each sexual or physical.

statistics of drug misuse.

a history of anxiety, unhappiness, or each extraordinary intellectual sickness.

Types of trauma and PTSD

Military struggle, toddler maltreatment or neglect, racism, injuries, natural disasters, tragedies in a single's very very own existence, or acts of violence are only a few of the horrifying conditions that may match away someone with trauma or PTSD signs and symptoms and symptoms and signs and signs and symptoms.

PTSD amongst former provider people

Too many veterans find that after serving within the army, they should cope with PTSD symptoms. It's feasible that transitioning out of the military can be difficult for you. Or you can have continual tension, enjoy emotionally numb and disconnected, be at the verge of panicking, or maybe erupt. However, it's miles critical to apprehend which you're not on my own and that there are various strategies you could use to control nightmares and flashbacks, further to emotions of despair, fear, or guilt, and reclaim your sense of control. We're going to speak greater about it in depth later in this ebook.

Trauma on a intellectual and emotional diploma

You may additionally additionally had been traumatized if you underwent a string of specifically annoying situations that made you enjoy powerless and out of manipulate emotionally. Psychological trauma regularly has formative years origins, however any incident that shatters your revel in of security can traumatize you, whether or not or no longer or now not or no longer it is an twist of destiny, an harm, the surprising loss of a loved one, bullying, home violence, or a profoundly humiliating come upon. Whether the trauma passed off years within the past or truly the day prior to this, you can recover from the damage, regain your experience of protection, and get on along with your existence.

Sexual attack or rape

You may also additionally experience nightmares, flashbacks, and distinctive distressing memories because of the trauma of being raped or sexually attacked, leaving you feeling terrified, embarrassed, and on my own. In spite of the way terrible you could feel right now, it's far important to recognize which you were not at fault for what came about and that you could reclaim your experience of safety, self assurance, and self confidence.

Racial trauma

Trauma related to racism results from witnessing it as abuse, injustice, or prejudice. Your enjoy of fee might be broken, that could cause anxiety, despair, continual stress, immoderate blood strain, disordered consuming, drug misuse, or even PTSD symptoms like hypervigilance, pessimism, and mood swings. But you could decorate your resilience and protect your intellectual health.

How does complicated PTSD (CPTSD) art work?

Oftentimes, PTSD is notion to be a great deal less severe than complicated positioned up-annoying pressure sickness (CPTSD or C-PTSD). It results from repeated exposure to disturbing conditions. For example, years of regular domestic abuse might possibly purpose CPTSD if you have been raised in an abusive home. This contamination may additionally moreover affect the ones who have endured repeated trauma thru slavery or one-of-a-type types of abuse.

Many of the identical PTSD symptoms, which embody hypervigilance, flashbacks, and emotional numbness, may also be present in CPTSD patients, similarly to:

Ideas which may be detrimental to you. You struggle persistent emotions of insignificance and excessive humiliation.

Emotional manage problems. You revel in robust feelings, experience too touchy, and battle to govern your anger. Dissociation, or the belief of being reduce off out of your environment, can also stand up.

Relationships are hard. You have a difficult hassle making or preserving love connections and friendships. It's fashionable to feel by myself.

Chapter 2: Complex Post Traumatic Strain Sickness

PTSD is a highbrow health illness this is the end result of a disturbing occasion. People regularly accomplice it with warfare veterans – someone flashing lower lower returned to the Afghan warfare due to the truth they have been because of way of a automobile backfiring, for instance. But, really, all and sundry who has suffered trauma is vulnerable to PTSD. And, steady with the World Health Organization, round 70% of humans enjoy as a minimum one traumatic occasion of their existence. Research suggests that without a doubt underneath 6% of those human beings will increase PTSD.

Everyone's revel in of PTSD is first rate, however human beings with the situation might also furthermore have routine recollections or nightmares related to the worrying event, they'll have distressing and intrusive thoughts approximately it, and they may be jumpy and without trouble startled. "Avoidance" is part of the situation, too.

People with PTSD may additionally additionally avoid humans or places that remind them of the trauma. Or they'll try and avoid the reminiscence by the usage of using the utilization of medication or alcohol.

The circumstance can severely have an effect on a person's relationships and is often related to eating issues, substance abuse, melancholy and suicidal behaviour.

How complicated PTSD is particular

In complicated PTSD, the trauma isn't always a one-off occasion, but a few detail repeated and sustained, which incorporates torture, home violence or early life abuse.

Complex PTSD consists of the identical symptoms and signs of PTSD, plus extra signs and symptoms and symptoms and symptoms called disturbance in self-organisation. Disturbance in self-business agency refers to problems in regulating feelings (for instance, feeling numb or having sudden anger outbursts), feeling remote from others, and having extremely horrible perspectives about your self.

Complex PTSD isn't as not unusual as PTSD, but it appears especially massive among particular agencies of human beings, together with refugees and people who enjoy psychosis.

The global trauma questionnaire has been superior as a self-report measure in particular designed to seize the additional signs of complex PTSD. The difference amongst PTSD and complex PTSD has been showed in over forty research and inside the course of 15 precise international places. A have a have a observe regarding nearly 1,seven-hundred doctors from 76 worldwide places positioned that, however versions in ethnicity and nationality, medical medical medical doctors had been capable of efficiently diagnose and distinguish among PTSD and complicated PTSD.

In the UK, complex PTSD is officially diagnosed through manner of every the NHS and the British Psychological Society, and famous highbrow health charities, which include Mind, strive to inform human beings approximately this new assessment.

The National Institute for Health and Care Excellence, which in England is in fee of publishing countrywide recommendations and recommendation to beautify fitness and social care, has no longer however advanced hints especially for complex PTSD. But numerous remedies (though in their early tiers) are being advanced.

How it's treated

In the meantime, folks that experience complex PTSD are being furnished the equal vintage treatments for PTSD. While such remedies have installed to be effective to an extent, they want to be provided for an extended length, have to be observed with the useful resource of more big guide and supplemented with more recovery approaches focusing mainly at the disturbance in self-organization organization signs and symptoms.

Usual treatments for PTSD that the NHS gives in England encompass trauma-centered cognitive behavioural treatment (CBT) and eye-movement desensitisation and reprocessing (EMDR).

Trauma-centered CBT can assist humans manage their complicated PTSD. Trauma-centered CBT includes eight to 12 weekly durations in which you find out how trauma will have an effect to your body and which strategies are beneficial to address signs, which consist of flashbacks.

EMDR is also offered as a direction of eight to 12 durations, in which you could try to don't forget info of the trauma on the same time as making eye moves, typically with the aid of the usage of following the motion of your therapist's finger. Both those remedies, on the equal time as powerful, contain considering the trauma and so may be pretty distressing.

Treatments which have multiple issue are the ones which might be more promising for managing complex PTSD signs. For example, a take a look at completed within the Netherlands placed that an in depth 8-day treatment programme combining particular strategies together with EMDR and bodily interest notably decreased signs and symptoms of each PTSD and complicated PTSD.

If you enjoy you can advantage from trauma-targeted treatment, or would like to speak approximately any symptoms and symptoms which you might be experiencing, you could communicate on your clinical health practitioner or, within the UK, refer your self for evaluation to an NHS psychological treatments company (IAPT) with out a referral from a GP.

Chapter 3: Facts About Post Traumatic Stress Disorder

PTSD facts

Clinical PTSD can amplify in as much as at least one-1/three of men and women who enjoy as regardless of the fact that they're now not capable of respire, as is the state of affairs with excessive COVID-19 times. According to investigate, the health center enjoy—feeling out of region, scared, and prefer you are drowning—is devastating.

Numerous survivors of septic shock and severe sepsis moreover point out having PTSD. The infection and people who have it are unfortunately the state of affairs of severa misconceptions.

Here are some statistics on PTSD.

1. About six Americans out of each a hundred could have PTSD at some point.

The U.S. Department of Veterans Affairs estimates that every 12 months, 12 million human beings inside the united states of america of the usa be thru PTSD. With 36.6% of PTSD sufferers reporting excessive signs and signs, 33.1% reporting slight signs and symptoms, and 30.2% reporting mild signs and symptoms, the severity of the disease appears to be equally disbursed.

2. The evaluation of PTSD have become simplest made officially 40 two years ago.

Prior to its inclusion inside the Diagnostic and Statistical Manual of the American Psychiatric Association in 1980, PTSD had no formal analysis. Even later—in 1992—come to be required for the World Health Organization to function it to the International Classification of Diseases.

three. The infection isn't always definitely associated with warfare and overt trauma.

Since humankind's evolution, PTSD has existed. It have grow to be known as struggle exhaustion, fight neurosis, shell shock, and great phrases throughout times of battle. These phrases, however, excluded people who evolved PTSD from exceptional motives, at the facet of being exposed to conflict, natural failures, trauma, abuse, or overlook. They furthermore limited the state of affairs to individuals who had served in conflict.

Another factor that might result in PTSD is a crucial illness, particularly one that is being treated in an extensive care unit (ICU). People with highbrow fitness problems, scary reminiscences of scientific emergencies, or who're sedated with capsules that could reason terrifying delusions or hallucinations are even more at chance.

4. Symptoms also can appear in caregivers.

Trauma influences more than simply the person who's experiencing it, whether or not or no longer it is thru violence or infection. Because of what happened to their cherished ones, caregivers may additionally get PTSD. Although experts are unsure of the right mechanism, pressure might be to play a key detail. According to a have a look at, greater than 70% of the accomplice and children and buddies of folks that were seriously ill confirmed signs and symptoms and symptoms and signs of despair. In some one-of-a-kind examine, it have come to be proven that mother and father of significantly sick children had more fees of PTSD and somatic symptoms (which encompass complications and exhaustion).

Who is more at danger amongst caregivers?

People who have formerly struggled with anxiety, depression, or different disturbing sports activities can be more likely to acquire PTSD.

5. After a trauma, now not every person develops PTSD.

Statistics display screen that 20% of survivors of catastrophic sports get PTSD, on the equal time as not all men and women who encounter traumatic activities do. Why is unknown to specialists. Even despite the fact that severa humans had the same events, truely one also can have the signs and symptoms and symptoms of PTSD.

People have a discounted danger of growing PTSD in the occasion that they:

enlist the beneficial resource of friends, own family, or help networks

Acquire the self belief to in reality receive their reaction to a painful enjoy.

Develop a coping mechanism that will help you get through and take a look at from a painful revel in.

however feeling afraid, are prepared and able to react to disturbing conditions as they take location.

If one of the following takes place, there may be an multiplied risk:

is more excessive

Has violence

spans a large amount of time

consists of hurting oneself Causes a cherished one to pass away

6. The signs and symptoms do no longer seem proper now.

Following a demanding occurrence, it is not unusual to have right now emotions of anxiety, melancholy, jitteriness, or disarray. Acute stress disorder is the not unusual call for this. The following want to occur inner at least one month of the annoying incident so you can be recognized with PTSD. Ideally, there can be:

Reliving the incident is one indication of re-experiencing.

When you retreat or keep away from a scenario that problems you and can bring about trauma-related signs, that is one avoidance signal.

Two arousal/reactivity signs and symptoms and symptoms, such irritation and a experience of unease

Having hassle focusing or dozing are cognition and temper troubles.

7. PTSD can also bring about bodily symptoms.

The majority people are aware that PTSD may additionally additionally result in tension and melancholy, but it can additionally damage bodily. The following are a number of the maximum standard bodily PTSD symptoms and symptoms:

a upward push in blood stress

coronary coronary coronary heart rate going up

Fatigue

muscle tenseness

Nausea

joint pain

Headaches

Back ache and other aches and pains

eight. There is remedy.

There is preference if you or a loved one gets PTSD. There isn't always any acknowledged remedy for PTSD, even though for a few people, it may be controlled to the element that signs recur once in a while or by no means in any respect. However, if you do start to experience symptoms and signs and symptoms all another time, PTSD remedy can be in a function that will help you control them and perhaps even train you a way to keep away from the triggers that began out them.

Talk therapy, usually known as cognitive remedy, is the maximum broadly used remedy for PTSD. You can find out proscribing beliefs and anxieties about the trauma reoccurring with the resource of working with a therapist. You can discover ways to deal with the ones sensations after spotting the false thoughts.

Behavior remedy referred to as exposure therapy includes intentionally exposing oneself to stimuli on the equal time as in a steady environment. Your therapist may stroll you via the event and help you come up with coping mechanisms for the ugly emotions.

Exposure is a treatment this is combined with eye motion desensitization and reprocessing (EMDR). Your mind learns the way to reprocess the inputs and your feelings by way of practicing eye actions and being exposed on your triggers.

Drugs that deal with melancholy, anxiety, and sleeplessness moreover aid in controlling the signs and symptoms and symptoms and signs and symptoms of PTSD. While a few humans exceptional require the medicine even as they will be in treatment, others require it longer.

Assistance with PTSD

There is help to be had in case you or a cherished one is suspected of getting PTSD. Speak up is the initial step. Consult your loved ones. Someone you recognize who has PTSD is probably able to direct you to the same services they did. You want to are seeking out recommendation out of your primary care physician as well, when you consider that they could advise a set or therapist. There are opportunity opportunities if you do not have a family doctor or experience which you aren't receiving the care you require. Keep attempting. PTSD is controllable.

Chapter 4: Military Veterans With Ptsd

Too many veterans find out that handling the effects of placed up-stressful stress disease after leaving the navy is tough. However, there are steps you may do proper away to start feeling better.

Knowing the way to deal with PTSD in squaddies

Are you finding it difficult to acclimate to life after the military? Do you typically experience on side, like you are approximately to panic or scream, or, as a substitute, do you feel emotionally numb and reduce off from your family? Do you think you can ever sense like yourself all yet again?

These continual symptoms of put up-annoying strain illness are a ordinary experience for some distance too many veterans (PTSD). Living with untreated PTSD is difficult, and the extended VA wait intervals make it simple to lose choice. However, at the equal time as you anticipate scientific attention, you may start to enjoy higher in recent times. There are numerous subjects you may do to useful resource on your recuperation from PTSD and emerge even extra effective than in advance than.

What brings on PTSD?

The state of affairs known as publish-demanding stress sickness (PTSD), regularly called shell surprise or battle pressure, develops after a completely worrying incident or a life-threatening state of affairs. After such an incidence, it's far regular in your mind and body to be in marvel, but when your worried device remains "caught," this regular response turns into PTSD.

Your apprehensive tool may react to annoying conditions in instinctive or reflexive techniques:

When you need to defend oneself or face up to the chance of a warfare scenario, you mobilize, regularly called "fight or flight." Your strength and response time boom due to your heart beating extra fast, your blood pressure developing, and your muscle companies turning into tighter. When a risk is not there, your irritating tool relaxes you, bringing your coronary coronary heart rate and blood strain lower lower returned to normal tiers.

When you are under too much stress in a condition, you may in all likelihood emerge as motionless and remain "stuck" despite the fact that the threat has surpassed. You aren't capable of permit skip of the incident, and your stressful tool is not able to return to its balanced state of affairs. That's PTSD.

Moving out of the mental and emotional fight sector you are despite the fact that dwelling in is important for PTSD restoration, as is supporting your demanding device in being "unstuck."

Veterans' PTSD symptoms

While PTSD signs and signs would in all likelihood appear inside hours or days after a annoying incidence, they are able to every now and then take months or possibly years to take location after a deployment. There are 4 symptom clusters for PTSD, albeit each veteran's PTSD manifests in a one in every of a kind manner:

Recurrent, bothersome reminiscences of the annoying incident, collectively with unsettling thoughts, nightmares, and flashbacks when you experience the feeling that the event is habitual. Reminders of the trauma can also cause strong emotional and bodily reactions in you, together with coronary coronary heart palpitations, panic attacks, and uncontrollable shaking.

excessive aversion to definitely anybody, anywhere, or whatever you find out with the terrible incident in your memory. This includes events and those as nicely. Losing interest in regular obligations and chickening out from pals and circle of relatives are examples of this.

Exaggeratedly pessimistic attitudes approximately oneself or the outside international, in addition to chronic feelings of dread, guilt, or shame, are examples of poor alterations for your thoughts and temper. You must have a look at a decline to your ability to feel properly.

Being constantly on defend, jumpy, and emotionally reactive as visible via using infection, rage, unstable conduct, troubles falling asleep, problem focusing, and hypervigilance (stepped forward alertness).

Suicide prevention for PTSD- infantrymen

Suicidal mind are regularly professional through soldiers with PTSD. Suicidal mind aren't someone fault, and that they do no longer endorse that you are insane, helpless, or defective.

PTSD danger factors

Although the reasons why a few troops have PTSD and others do no longer are unknown, it's far diagnosed that the superiority will growth with the range of deployments and the depth of the battle you participated in. This is comprehensible for the reason that many PTSD symptoms, together with hypervigilance, hyperawareness, and adrenaline-spurred fast reflexes, assisted in your survival all through deployment. Only now which you're lower back at home do you recognise how wrong the ones remarks are.

It won't display up speedy to learn how to "unstuck," but if you technique it daily, you will rapid take a look at outcomes. Additionally, on the same time as you growth coping mechanisms for your wartime pressure, you may additionally be growing success-enhancing abilities that pass nicely past PTSD restoration.

Treating PTSD among veterans

Step 1: Get shifting.

Exercise on a regular foundation has extended been essential for PTSD warriors. Exercise assist you to take away more adrenaline, release endorphins, and raise your temper. Additionally, thru the usage of paying near interest for your body whilst you exercise, you could even help your neural tool in breaking unfastened from its immobility pressure response.

Running, swimming, playing basketball, or even dancing are examples of rhythmic bodily games that make use of each your legs and arms. These physical sports work great at the same time as you are taking study of approaches your body feels as you bypass in region of your mind.

Try to be aware of small data, which incorporates the sound of your toes at the floor, the rhythm of your respiration, or the sensation of the wind to your pores and pores and skin. Many PTSD patients discover that activities like mountain climbing, boxing, weightlifting, and martial arts help them attention on their bodily motions due to the fact in the event that they do not, they danger injuring themselves. Try to exercising for half of-hour or more each day, or if it's more available, 3 10-minute bursts of activity are certainly as useful.

The blessings of being outdoor

Hiking, camping, mountain biking, mountain climbing, whitewater rafting, and skiing are examples of outdoor activities in nature that allow you to test your experience of vulnerability and ease the transition lower lower back into everyday lifestyles.

Look for network organizations that offer possibilities for group-constructing or outside enjoyment, or, within the US, have a have a look at Sierra Club Military Outdoors. This software gives possibilities for provider contributors, veterans, and their households to get out of doors and glide.

Step 2: Control your frightened system in your very own

PTSD could make you revel in defenseless and inclined. But you couldn't be aware of how a lot have an effect on you absolutely have over your neurological device. These pointers will let you in converting your arousal gadget and calming your self while you feel indignant, involved, or out of manage.

Conscious respiratory. Simply take 60 breaths, targeting every "out" breath, to right away loosen up oneself in any situation. Alternatively, you may workout this guided conscious respiration meditation.

Sensory records. Similar to how specific scents, loud noises, or the sensation of sand for your clothing can also right away take you lower back to the battlefield, sensory enter also can suddenly loosen up you. Everybody reacts a piece bit in a brilliant manner, so try severa subjects to look what fits you the exquisite. When you replicate for your deployment, what did you switch to for solace on the surrender of the day? Maybe it turn out to be looking at family photographs? Or perhaps gambling your favorite track, or smelling your preferred cleaning cleansing cleaning soap? Or probably right away caressing an animal calms you down?

Emotional reconnection It's not unusual to want to overlook or avoid going through the stuff you went thru in war. But the problem is that getting rid of such reminiscences might not honestly lead them to disappear. The mind, images, and desires need to even worsen and greater obtrusive even as you try to repress them. Reconnecting together with your emotions is the fine manner to get better and move on. Although taking this step is probably daunting, you can learn how to enjoy even the maximum ugly emotions without being too beaten.

Make a "secure" area

You already apprehend that the arena can be lethal at instances since you survived a battle sector. The trouble with PTSD is that it gives you the affect that hazard remains there no matter the fact that it isn't always. You may additionally moreover have a strong spot to withdraw to while you want to unwind, meditate, or paintings via unsightly reviews with the useful resource of constructing your very non-public steady vicinity (ideally somewhere close by and sensible).

The regular spot want to be a quiet, strong area with constrained get right of entry to— someplace you could loosen up without disturbing approximately out of doors threats or intruders. Your place of business or mattress room might be the region. Or it may be a much off place of your outdoor or every other outdoor place. Make positive it's tranquil and orderly (no worrying workplace work, unfinished tasks, or messes to distract you). You might also want to need to consist of objects that calm you down and make you experience correct, like plant life, circle of relatives pics, or posters of your preferred locations.

Step 3: Connect with others Face-to-face verbal exchange could now not typically require a whole lot of speaking. Finding someone who will keep out with you or concentrate to you without passing judgment is important for any soldier laid low with

PTSD. Your large one-of-a-kind, a member of your own family, a close to acquaintance from the army, or a friend from the civilian global may be that person. Or strive:

Donating it sluggish to a motive that subjects to you or helping out a stranger. This is a great approach to experience extra linked to others and take lower again your electricity.

Joining a assist group for PTSD. Making pals with different veterans going via similar troubles would possibly in all likelihood make you experience less by myself and offer you beneficial recommendation on a way to deal with signs and similarly your rehabilitation.

Interacting with the general public

Since they've now not served in the army or professional what you've got were given have been given, you may experience that the civilians for your lifestyles cannot relate to you. People may also select out to difficult emotions and be supportive even though they've got not lengthy beyond via the same real topics. It's crucial that the individual you switch to is aware of you, is a terrific listener, and might provide solace.

You are not required to talk about your military company. It's completely best if you're no longer prepared to speak approximately the specifics of what happened. You can specific your feelings without giving an extensive narrative of what passed off.

Inform the opportunity character of your desires and the way they'll help you. That can also virtually propose spending time with you and listening, or it is able to recommend taking motion. Someone else knowledge your emotional enjoy might be comforting.

Your friends and own family need that will help you. For them, listening isn't a problem however as an opportunity a totally happy risk to provide assist.

Step 4: Look after your body.

The bodily toll that PTSD symptoms like sleeplessness, rage, hassle concentrating, and jumpiness may have to your body will ultimately have an effect on your chosen fitness. Because of this, it's vital to appearance after your wishes.

Whether it is caffeine, cocaine, violent video games, unstable using, or volatile sports activities activities sports, you can be tempted to interests and conduct that boom your adrenaline degrees. That feels normal after being in a conflict area. However, if you could pick out out what those cravings truely are, you could pick out better actions so that you can soothe and guard each your body and your thoughts.

Enjoy a few downtime. Relaxation strategies like massage, meditation, or yoga can enhance your sleep, assist you revel in extra at peace, and reduce stress. They can also reduce the signs and symptoms of sadness and tension.

Look for wholesome strategies to permit off frustration. Punching a bag, kicking a pillow, going for a brisk run, making a track alongside to loud tune, or locating a quiet vicinity to scream aloud are all effective techniques to launch strain.

Maintain your body with a nutritious weight loss plan. Include components like fatty salmon, flaxseed, and walnuts to your weight loss plan due to the fact that they embody omega-3s, which may be essential for intellectual fitness. Limit substances which might be processed, fried, sugary, and excessive in sensitive carbohydrates due to the truth they may make mood swings and electricity swings worse.

Get hundreds of relaxation. Lack of sleep makes human beings more indignant, irritable, and moody. Each night, try and get 7 to 9 hours of suitable sleep. Make your bedroom as darkish and silent as you could, set up a non violent night time time recurring (listen to calming tune, take a warm bathe, or take a look at a few thing slight and tasty), and transfer off displays at least an hour in advance than going to mattress.

AVOID DRUG AND DRAUGHTS (which consist of nicotine). It is probably lovely to use tablets and alcohol to block out unsightly recollections and go to sleep. However, drug dependancy can exacerbate PTSD signs and symptoms. In the same manner, cigarettes. Stop smoking if you could, and get treatment if you have ingesting or drug issues.

Step five: Address dreams, intrusive mind, and flashbacks

Flashbacks are generally related to each auditory and seen reminiscences of combat for veterans with PTSD. It's vital to reassure your self that the revel in is not taking place proper now as it appears to be repeating itself. This is what trauma professionals communicate over with as "dual reputation."

Dual awareness is the information that your "experiencing self" and your "watching self" are terrific from every other. You enjoy the trauma as although it's miles going on right now, it really is one element of your inner emotional reality. On the opportunity issue, you will probably check your surroundings and apprehend which you are secure. Despite what you are going thru, you're aware that the trauma occurred within the beyond. Now, it's miles not taking region.

Declare to yourself (aloud or to your mind) that irrespective of feeling as even though the trauma is taking location right now, you can appearance spherical and apprehend that you are solid.

When you start to have flashbacks or wake up from a nightmare, follow this honest script: I'm recalling a [traumatic incident] and I feel [panicked, afraid, overwhelmed, etc.], however as I appearance round, I apprehend that neither the event nor I am in threat in the intervening time.

What do you be conscious as you look spherical? (name the location in which you are, the current date, and three property you spot whilst you go searching).

To help you return to the existing, try tapping your palms on the same time as you offer an purpose in the back of what you notice.

How to "floor" oneself all through a flashback: If you experience like you'll dissociate or have a flashback, use your senses to convey your self lower lower again to the winning. Try numerous matters to look what fits you the excellent.

Movement. Actively pass round (jump up and down, run in region, and lots of others.); rub your palms together; shake your head

Touch. Play with worry beads or a stress ball, splash bloodless water on your face, keep a bit of ice, touch or keep onto a secure object, pinch yourself, or do any aggregate of these.

Sight. Blink firmly and fast, then go searching and list what you be aware.

Sound. Play loud track, clap or stamp your feet, and communicate to yourself to reassure your self which you are secure and can be incredible.

Smell. Smell a scent that brings again nice recollections or a few detail that connects you to the existing, which encompass mouthwash, espresso, or the perfume or cologne your large one-of-a-kind wears.

Taste. Take a strong mint or bite a few gum, consume some factor sour or warmth, then sip a few cool juice or water.

Chapter 5: What Does Ptsd In Kids Mean?

When a infant endures particularly demanding activities, post-worrying stress disease can also increase. Children commonly get better from pressure speedy. However, they may have publish-annoying pressure sickness if they exhibit symptoms and signs and symptoms for extra than a month. This also can arise following a worrying occasion which incorporates an damage, the loss of life or drawing near death of a cherished one, or violent behavior.

PTSD also can be introduced on by using using:

Being a witness to or a sufferer of crime or violence

Natural (like floods) or guy-made (like earthquakes) screw ups

Maltreatment may be bodily, emotional, or sexual.

Unsafe the usage of

Severe contamination of a relative or near buddy

Signs of PTSD

Your toddler's relationships and manner of life can also go through due to positioned up-stressful stress. Children with submit-traumatic stress disease may additionally additionally show off the following signs:

nightmares and trouble slumbering

now not feeling or questioning positively

getting indignant at the same time as the trauma is added up

playing out or replaying the annoying occasion over and over to your head

mood tantrums and irritability

Constant melancholy or severe, ongoing worry

Lack of optimism and performing helpless or a long way flung without trouble being startled

denying that the annoying event ever occurred

heading off the ones or locations which can be related to the annoying event

When looking a little one displaying PTSD signs and symptoms, you need to workout warning.   Attention-deficit/hyperactivity sickness can be pressured with restlessness in a child who moreover struggles with corporation or paying attention.

When to call your scientific health practitioner

You should contact your medical doctor if your little one has lengthy beyond via a demanding enjoy while:

Friends, own family, or perhaps teachers are alarmed through the use of your little one's behavior.

They begin showing excessive tension, fear, or anger toward themselves and extraordinary people.

For three or greater days in a row, your child hasn't had sufficient to eat or sleep, and that they feel or act out of control.

They have hallucinations, which incorporate seeing or listening to things that different people can't.

The following advice can be used to useful resource and cope with a toddler who has PTSD:

Give your infant some time to regulate at the same time as being understanding, loving, and supportive.

Be careful no longer to deal with the child differently or considerably regulate their time desk.

When they're prepared and in their private manner, permit your infant speak the incident. Encourage them and congratulate them on their resilience in enduring the demanding revel in.

If your toddler is vintage enough, permit them to make selections which have an effect on them a good way to help them expand self-self perception. Tell them their feelings are normal and not "loopy," and reassure them of this.

Regressive behavior have to not be criticized or penalized. If your infant has professional big strain, you want to be information within the event that they favor to sleep with the lights on or deliver their favored filled animal with them to mattress.

In some occasions, it is able to be useful to embody a traumatized toddler in a help group for trauma survivors.

Assure them that the worrying event changed into now not their fault and encourage them to particular any guilt they may be experiencing.

If your toddler shows self-damage or suicide, speak with a professional.

Keep in touch with your toddler's caregivers, along with their teachers.

The difference among PTSD in kids and adults

Similar to the way it influences youngsters, PTSD additionally influences adults. Both the reasons and the symptoms are the identical. However, adults are extra capable than kids to speak approximately their feelings and reviews.

Children with PTSD are also much more likely than adults to bodily retaliate (together with screaming) once they enjoy fear or tension. Children conflict more than adults to without a doubt take delivery of that the annoying occasion will not recur.

PTSD treatment for youngsters

The nature, timing, and quantity of the child's exposure to the worrying occasion all play a position in how PTSD in children is generally handled. Even with the assist and aid of pals and circle of relatives, some children may additionally have hassle recovering from a disturbing event. Consult a consultant who is licensed to address trauma the use of proof-based totally practices.

Among the alternatives for treating PTSD in youngsters are:

Cognitive-behavioral remedy is a behavioral method that aids in converting terrible or poor mind into favorable ones.

Play remedy: Younger youngsters who are not able to deal with trauma on an character basis can benefit from play remedy. Eye movement desensitization and reprocessing therapy (EMDR): Anyone of any age can advantage from this technique. Combining cognitive remedy with directed eye actions is how the remedy works.

Medication: Your doctor may additionally advocate treatment to address excessive tension and depressive signs and symptoms and signs. Once those signs and signs and symptoms subside, the medication is stopped, and your infant will preserve with remedy until they'll be honestly recovered.

Children's PTSD Prevention

Avoiding conditions in which your toddler ought to possibly revel in massive pressure is the principle technique for preventing PTSD. By keeping off violence and different kinds of abuse further to restricting the damage that unavoidable failures reason to youngsters, you may lessen the probability that a infant will enjoy trauma.

How can dad and mom help?

Here are a few matters you could do if your little one has skilled trauma:

Make your baby sense solid. They may want to likely require extra hobby, solace, and care from you for some time.

Relax your infant. By doing so, They are welcome to take a few deep breaths with you. As you keep in mind amount to 3, inhale. Exhale as you count to 5.

Do sports activities you each revel in as a couple. The happy emotions that manifestly assist youngsters recharge can be greater difficult to revel in after trauma. Play, snicker, soak up nature, create paintings or track, and put together food. These hobbies can help your little one turn out to be more resilient and masses much less burdened.

Assurances for your infant. Inform them that they will overcome this. You're to be had to help, too.

Tell your little one's physician approximately the reminiscences they have had. Obtain a recommendation for a highbrow fitness expert (like a psychiatrist, psychologist, or intellectual fitness counselor who makes a speciality of trauma treatment).

Inform the instructor of the trauma your child has skilled. PTSD can also make it tougher for youngsters to pay interest on their schoolwork. When your toddler goals greater assist or more time to complete their schoolwork, request it.

Chapter 6: How To Assist Kids Who Are Having Problem Coping While A Discern Has Ptsd

You may additionally find out that your children react to you otherwise in case you're a determine with PTSD. The adjustments and signs and symptoms they word might be past their comprehension. Discover the standard reactions that kids have to a discern's PTSD and examine advice on how you can assist them in dealing with it better.

How Could a Parent's PTSD Symptoms Affect Their Kids?

Family contributors may be impacted with the resource of a number of PTSD signs and symptoms. Here are some instances of the way numerous PTSD symptoms and signs would likely have an impact on extra younger human beings.

Symptoms resurfacing

People with PTSD frequently "re-experience" horrible research in their goals or reminiscences. It would possibly seem to take area out of nowhere and display up suddenly. Strong sentiments of disappointment, remorse, worry, or wrath regularly accompany these signs and symptoms. It's viable for an event to be so effective that you could consider the trauma is reoccurring. Both you and your children may additionally find out those signs and symptoms and signs and symptoms and signs and symptoms to be frightful. Children could not recognise what's going on or why it's far taking region. They can worry for his or her mother and father or fear that they may no longer be taken care of.

Symptoms of withdrawal and avoidance

People with PTSD try and keep away from thinking about the incident because the symptoms of re-experiencing are so distressing. Avoiding situations and gadgets that purpose your PTSD also can be a method. You won't enjoy like performing activities which you as soon as located a laugh, which include attending your little one's occasion or the films. Having excellent feelings might be tough for PTSD patients. You might also revel in "near off" from your circle of relatives and youngsters. The upshot is that children can anticipate the determine with PTSD does not care approximately them.

Signs of multiplied arousal

Anxiousness and being "on factor" are commonplace among humans with PTSD. You ought to have problems falling asleep or focusing when you have PTSD. You might be grumpy or livid pretty a few the time. You must have a susceptible belly or fear excessively about your protection or the protection of these you want. It is easy to understand how the ones problems might have an effect on family human beings. A decide may additionally pop out as nasty or livid within the occasion that they act grumpy, for example. Children also can query whether or not or no longer the figure loves them for the motive that they do no longer recognize the PTSD signs and symptoms and signs and symptoms.

How do children react to conditions?

The reactions of a infant are right away correlated with PTSD symptoms and signs and symptoms and signs in mother and father. Typical responses from youngsters consist of:

A teenager may also attempt to set up a reference to a figure thru appearing and feeling precisely like them. Some of the determine's PTSD symptoms and signs and symptoms may additionally additionally arise in the little one.

If a discern has PTSD, a baby need to step in to act as the grownup. The teen shows an excessive amount of maturity for their age.

Some children do no longer get emotional help in any respect. Later interpersonal issues, educational troubles, sorrow, and tension (venture, worry) can all end quit result from this.

Veterans' kids who have PTSD

According to numerous studies, PTSD-affected veterans' kids are more likely to conflict socially, academically, and with conduct problems. Their parents recognize them to be extra depressed, worried, opposed, and hyperactive than youngsters of Veterans with out PTSD. A discern's PTSD may also be related to home violence and competitive conduct in kids, consistent with a few studies. However, it is extensive to undergo in mind that almost all of veterans live in peaceful families.

Secondary traumatization and emotional issues

Some youngsters of PTSD-affected fight veterans experience greater unhappiness and tension than kids of PTSD-free non-fight veterans. Although it's far uncommon, kids every so often have signs and symptoms and signs and symptoms which is probably similar to their parents'. For instance, a toddler ought to dream approximately their traumatized dad and mom.

Due to seeing their parents' illnesses, children might also get PTSD signs and symptoms and symptoms and symptoms. For example, a teenager who is stressful about her decide's troubles can also furthermore conflict to pay hobby in elegance. "Secondary traumatization" refers to the results of a discern's PTSD symptoms and signs and symptoms on a infant.

Since there may be violence in sure households in which a parent suffers from PTSD, the children also can revel in their private PTSD symptoms and signs and symptoms and symptoms because of the violence. If a decide can not provide emotional help, a baby's PTSD symptoms and signs and symptoms and signs also can worsen.

Teenage years can also see issues persist.

The signs and symptoms and signs and symptoms and symptoms of their mother and father' PTSD may also moreover have an impact on their teenagers. One take a look at contrasted the teenage youngsters of fight veterans with non-combat veterans in Vietnam. The teens of Vietnam War combat veterans had terrible attitudes in the direction of their dads and inside the direction of education. They had been a lot less creative and felt greater melancholy and anxiety. Additionally, their mothers seemed them as having greater tricky behaviors.

They behaved at school and in social conditions similarly to non-Veteran youngsters, notwithstanding the reality that. This may be the case for the reason that dads on this research did now not have a right PTSD analysis. Overall, even as a decide Veteran has mental health troubles like PTSD, problems with teens are significantly much more likely.

Does Parental PTSD Affect Children?

Although it's miles unusual, it's far feasible for children to reveal PTSD signs and signs due to being tormented by their parents' signs. The results of trauma additionally may be handed down at some point of generations or from determine to little one. "Intergenerational transmission of trauma" is what this is known as. Families of Holocaust survivors from World War II have professional this. Families of battle veterans with PTSD have said experiencing it as well. How it absolutely works is as follows:

The anxiety of a teen worsens on the same time as his family maintains him quiet or instructs him to preserve his thoughts, emotions, or distressing occurrences to himself. If he discusses the trauma, he can begin to be involved that he's going to cause the parent's signs and symptoms. He need to remember some thing that become worse than what in fact happened almost approximately the figure.

Sometimes mother and father supply away too much information about what happened. As a stop result of seeing the ones horrible pictures, children may also begin to expose off their very very own unique set of PTSD symptoms and signs.

As a way to narrate to her dad and mom, a toddler may additionally begin to enjoy her decide's signs and symptoms.

Children can also moreover moreover recreate high-quality factors of the trauma because of the reality they have a look at their mother and father suffering to differentiate among the previous trauma and the existing.

How May I Help?

By the usage of the information in this e-book at the facet of various assets, mother and father may additionally moreover help kids. The functionality results of a determine's PTSD on children might be mentioned with own family contributors by using parents or professionals. Family people may moreover discover it useful to discover how worrying memories can be transferred from determine to youngster.

Educating youngsters about a parent's PTSD is a beneficial first step in assisting them in dealing with the state of affairs. Be careful no longer to offer the teen too many specifics approximately the occasion(s). The amount you talk will rely upon your infant's age and degree of adulthood. Children should be made to recognize that their ailments are not their fault. A counselor can also moreover offer recommendation to mother and father who want assistance in deciding what to say to their children.

Options for treatment

Various remedy options are available. Family counseling and individual treatment also are options for the Veteran or grownup with PTSD. In addition to supporting the PTSD-affected figure, circle of relatives treatment teaches special circle of relatives participants the way to fulfill their personal wishes.

According to the children's age, children also can gain from their very very personal treatment, which may be unique. Each own family is unique, so it is able to be hard to determine what kind of remedy, if any, to pursue. The most vital aspect is to manual each member of the family, especially the children, in expressing their needs.

Chapter 7: Post-Demanding Stress Disorder After Giving Starting

If you encounter traumatic sports activities on the same time as giving start or laboring, you can extend postnatal PTSD.

Here are some instances of traumatic incidents that would bring about postnatal PTSD:

A difficult being pregnant

A protracted and painful tough work

An unanticipated cesarean section

Emergency care, and extraordinary stunning, unexpected, and demanding shipping studies.

Some humans accept as real with that the advent of a modern day little one makes up for any stressful occasions. Or they may get hold of as real with that because of the reality they will be having a laugh as new parents, their annoying reminiscences will quickly be forgotten.

The courting you have were given collectively together along with your baby and the people on your life can also additionally moreover undergo because of the ones worrying activities.

If your being pregnant and delivery did now not cross as deliberate, you will probable revel in dissatisfied. If the delivery didn't move with out issues, you can moreover be dissatisfied with the scientific employees.

Your research may also additionally make you worried about having a 2nd toddler in the destiny, if you want to undergo a similar birthing machine.

Postnatal PTSD symptoms and symptoms and signs and symptoms

Among the commonplace postnatal PTSD signs and symptoms and symptoms are:

1.Experiencing a number of the trauma all over again. It can also incorporate:

Striking flashbacks (feeling that the trauma is going on proper now)

Disturbing thoughts and pics

Intense misery while reminded of the trauma in actual or symbolic methods in nightmares

Physical afflictions like ache, sweating, nauseousness, or trembling.

2. Feeling on issue or alert. It can also incorporate:

Anxiety signs and signs like panicking even as the trauma is remembered

Being effects upset or irritated.

Being on excessive alert, additionally referred to as "hypervigilance"

Finding it hard to go to sleep, even when there can be a threat of doing so

Acting irritable or aggressively

Being jumpy or effortlessly startled

Acting recklessly or self-destructively.

three. Avoidance of emotions or recollections

It might also embody:

Feeling such as you want to maintain busy to maintain from being reminded of the trauma

Having trouble recalling specifics of what occurred

Feeling reduce off from your feelings or emotionally numb

Feeling emotionally or physical numb, now not capable of explicit affection, and using alcohol or recreational pills to block out recollections.

four. Difficult mind and emotions

It may contain:

Having the have an effect on that nobody may be trusted and that no longer whatever is strong

Overwhelming feelings of anger, sadness, guilt, or disgrace

Feeling like no character is acquainted with

Blaming yourself for what passed off.

Postnatal PTSD remedies

For postnatal PTSD, you is probably given masses of treatments. Your medical doctor must bypass over these alternatives with you so that you can decide together at the tremendous direction of movement:

Speech remedy

Particular forms of speakme remedy function the number one PTSD treatments:

Cognitive behavioral remedy (CBT) with a trauma popularity, this is intended to address PTSD.

Reprocessing and desensitization of eye motion (EMDR). During this therapy, a therapist will direct your rhythmic eye moves as you don't forget the traumatic occasion. To stimulate the mind's statistics-processing device, the eye moves are meant. The purpose of the treatment is to hasten your readjustment and healing by way of supporting you in processing the worrying activities.

Medication

For the maximum element, PTSD itself isn't treated with remedy. However, there are some associated reasons which could spark off your medical scientific doctor to prescribe treatment to you:

PTSD is often located by way of the usage of way of hysteria and melancholy. For the treatment of those symptoms and signs, your medical medical doctor may additionally moreover prescribe medication.

To experience more sturdy and able to being involved on your little one, your medical doctor may also prescribe medicine.

There may be lengthy prepared lists to your region for speaking treatments. As you assume treatment, your medical medical doctor could probably recommend taking medicinal drug.

PTSD after childbirth: self-care

There are a few topics you could do to assist yourself on the identical time as managing the aftereffects of a demanding starting:

Discover your triggers

It's viable that particular reminiscences, conditions, or humans appear to carry decrease lower returned other signs and symptoms and signs like flashbacks. These may be precise subjects, like aromas, sounds, terms, locations, or positive genres of literature or movie, that function reminders of beyond trauma.

On crucial dates, a few humans locate life especially difficult. This should, for example, be a infant's birthday or the anniversary of every different demanding event.

Trust some different person.

It is probably hard if you need to be open with humans when you have postnatal PTSD. This will be a stop end result of your feeling no longer able to talk approximately what has occurred. To specific how you sense proper now, however, you do no longer have which will describe the trauma.

Talking to a chum or member of your circle of relatives may be useful. Alternatively, you'll probably want to talk with a representative like a clinical medical doctor or a skilled listener at a helpline.

Make time for your self

It's important to transport at your very non-public tempo because everyone reacts to trauma otherwise. It may not be useful, as an instance, to percentage your evaluations in advance than you are organized.

Try to be tolerant of your self. Please do no longer be hard on your self if you need a while and help to get over postnatal PTSD.

Attempt peer manual

Peer help brings collectively people with similar stories so that it will take note of and percentage every different's critiques. This includes attending an in-character peer help corporation for your network or signing up for a web organization like Mind's Side thru the use of Side.

Discover expert assistance

There are agencies that focus on providing steerage and help for postnatal PTSD, together with the Birth Trauma Association.

Maintain your bodily health.

It may be tough to manipulate postnatal PTSD. You may also anticipate it isn't feasible an extraordinary way to muster the strength to appearance after yourself. But whilst it's far viable, searching after your bodily health may want to have an impact on the way you revel in at the interior. Spending time out of doors, preserving a healthful food plan, and making an try and exercising are some examples of what may be beneficial.

Chapter 8: Getting Well After Sexual Trauma And Rape

It can make an effort to heal from the traumatic experience of being the sufferer of a sexual attack. The recuperation machine may be very painful further to being stressful. You undergo mental damage further to physical results from having been the sufferer of sexual violence. You want severa help from those close to you to rebuild your life, your sense of properly nicely well worth, and your functionality for recovery.

The Effects of Being Sexually Traumatized and Raped

Every 12 months, rape and sexual assault victims include women, younger girls, men, and boys everywhere in the global. You turn out to be damaged, afraid, by myself, and ashamed because of sexual trauma. The remaining effect can be that you consider the arena isn't a secure vicinity to be in due to flashbacks, nightmares, and jarring recollections. It might be difficult or not feasible for those who have professional sexual trauma to trust every body another time, along with themselves.

The affects of being a rape and sexual trauma victim frequently consist of you questioning whether or not or now not the following:

your judgment

esteem in the course of yourself

sanity

You can even take the blame to your moves and definitely anticipate which you are "broken items" or "filthy." Another grave repercussion of being raped or experiencing sexual trauma is that you could discover it tough to be in a dating because it feels volatile. Many sufferers of this type of abuse were so extensively traumatized via the occasion that they suffered from PTSD, melancholy, and top notch anxiety problems.

The sentiments of guilt, defectiveness, self-blame, and helplessness are nice symptoms and not actual reactions to a worrying incident. All of the aforementioned are common reactions to trauma. As a result, it's far vital which you get assist at the way to start the healing method and to reclaim your sense of accept as true with and safety, to be able to permit you to circulate on and lead as everyday a existence as viable.

Rape and sexual attack: Facts and Myths

One issue of the healing method is dispelling the myths approximately sexual violence. This covers each sufferer-blaming fable as well as numerous extra, which embody the subsequent:

Myth: You can understand ability rapists through the manner they act and appearance.

Fact: Because many rapists seem certainly normal, non-threatening, pleasant, and charming, it might be no longer viable to recognize them with the resource in their appearance or conduct.

Myth: You ought to not have idea the revel in have become that ugly in case you did no longer face up to the attack.

Fact: The tendency for sexual attack sufferers to "freeze" is a truth. Your body and mind close down due to being shocked. You find it hard to anticipate, talk, or skip due to this.

Myth: Anyone who changed into raped "called for it" because of how they behaved or how they dressed.

Fact: It is a longtime truth that rape is a "possibility" crime. According to research, rapists generally chose their sufferers due to the truth they'll be vulnerable, instead of due to their appearance or possibly their flirtatiousness.

Myth: Often, date rape is surely a false impression.

Fact: It is conventional for date rapists to offer a protection with the useful resource of putting forward that there has been a false impression or that the sexual attack turned into the forestall end end result of intoxication. However, research has validated that almost all of date rapists are without a doubt "repeat offenders," who prey at the inclined with the aid of way of supplying them with alcohol as a way to rape or sexually abuse their meant sufferers.

Myth: The idea that having intercourse with someone earlier than does no longer constitute "rape"

Fact: A person does no longer have "perpetual rights" on your body clearly because you gave your previous settlement to having intercourse with them. Your boyfriend, companion, or some other character forcing you to have sex with them constitutes "rape."

How to Get Well After Rape or Other Sexual Trauma

After experiencing rape or sexual trauma, there are actions you can do to assist your self heal and regain your lifestyles.

Step 1: Be prone with others.

Be honest with them and percent your reports. Because they enjoy it might cause them to revel in inclined and unclean to mention they were the patients of rape or exceptional sexual trauma, many victims find it quite hard to obtain this. Another problem is that you could in no way anticipate how someone you may percent your enjoy with will reply. You may want to probably surprise within the event that they may "choose" you or view you "in any other case". You could probable therefore trust that it might be a great deal less difficult to virtually downplay what took place and maintain it to your self. You is probably depriving yourself of the opportunity to get the assist and guide you require in case you made a decision on to maintain quiet, even though.

Reaching out to someone you may accept as genuine with is crucial. You should now not anticipate that by way of using preserving your revel in to your self, it did not honestly appear. You can not begin the "recuperation" manner by way of the usage of denying the truth, and burying your emotions will absolutely boom any existing disgrace you will be feeling. It can be frightening to open up, however doing so ought to "set you unfastened." In moderate of the foregoing, it's far essential that the individual making a decision to divulge heart's contents to approximately your terrible event is a person you may truly recollect because they may be sympathetic and useful even as maintaining their composure. You have to get in touch with a rape disaster hotline or an authorized therapist in case you do not experience like you may agree with every body.

It's important which you fight any emotions of powerlessness and loneliness you'll be experiencing. Any form of demanding occasion leaves you with feelings of vulnerability and weak point, consequently it is critical to steer yourself which you have numerous strengths and exquisite coping mechanisms to help you get via difficult instances. Helping others is a splendid way to regain your feel of energy. You can do this with the resource of donating a while, giving blood, lending a hand to a pal in want, or developing a donation for your selected charity.

You may join up for a help institution that aids one-of-a-kind rape, sexual attack, or trauma patients. Being part of a assist organization will assist you experience a good buy an awful lot less alienated and on my own whilst additionally presenting you with pointers on a manner to deal so that you can start down the route to restoration.

Step 2: Dealing with your emotions of guilt and humiliation

Even despite the fact that you'll be aware that you are not in charge for the sexual attack you skilled, it can be tough to dismiss any emotions of guilt or disgrace you is probably having. These feelings may additionally moreover come to be apparent right now after a rape or sexual attack, or they may take time to emerge. It's crucial to maintain in thoughts that if you encompass the reality of what sincerely occurred to you, it will likely be plenty simpler on the way to just accept the fact that you are not in any respect responsible for what happened and which you do now not have whatever to be embarrassed of.

You often revel in emotions of guilt and shame due to misconceptions like the following:

1 That you've got were given been attacked and that you couldn't prevent it. It is typically lot a great deal less difficult to reflect on what you likely did or did not do after an occurrence. Being sexually attacked sends your body and thoughts into marvel, making it hard with a view to count on rationally. It's not unusual for sufferers to explain how they "iced over" for the duration of rape or attack, that could be a everyday response to this form of trauma. It's critical to remind yourself that you tried your toughest given the times and that you could have prevented the sexual assault if you can have completed whatever.

2. That you "must not have" positioned your consider in someone. The notion that a acquainted person "violated" your accept as authentic with is the toughest issue to address after being sexually attacked. Because you may have overlooked the caution indicators, you could start to doubt yourself. This is high-quality normal, but it is important to comprehend that anybody who violates your sexual integrity is not a "real character." Your assailant, not you, is the simplest who have to be feeling "accountable," not you.

three. That you had been intoxicated and now not as careful as you have to were. Whatever the scenario, you've got been sexually assaulted, and it modified into your attacker's fault. It is the rapist who have to be held accountable for the attack on you because of the fact neither you nor every body else "requested" for it.

Step three: is to get prepared for distressing reminiscences and powerful flashbacks.

When you undergo a stressful state of affairs, it's miles regular in your body to go into "flight-or-flight" mode. Your frame returns to normal and calms down as soon due to the reality the "danger" ends. However, rape and sexual attack located someone's involved device into what is defined as a "kingdom of immoderate alert," which makes them greater willing. As many rape survivors revel in, it basically approach that you are hyper-alert to the smallest of stimuli. In specific within the path of the number one few months following a sexual assault, you may revel in nightmares, demanding reminiscences, and flashbacks. You run the danger of getting PTSD, which lengthens the length of the intrusive memories, nightmares, and flashbacks if the disturbing incident leaves your nervous tool permanently "stuck."

You can attempt the following to lessen your anxiety and tension because of the distressing flashbacks and reminiscences you experience after a sexual assault:

1 Be privy to any triggers and be prepared for them. The maximum not unusual triggers encompass locations related to rape or sexual attack, anniversary dates, and positive factors of hobby, sounds, and smells. Being prepared and in a more potent characteristic to take the required moves to relax once more with the useful resource of being aware about the triggers that might result in you having an frightening reaction might be the advantages of doing so.

2. Bear in mind that your body sends out "risk signs" even as it begins to enjoy threatened or below strain. This includes telltale symptoms like gasping for air, feeling tight, having racing thoughts, feeling quick of breath, feeling queasy, having warm flashes, and feeling nauseous.

3. In the occasion which you come across any of the aforementioned signs and symptoms, take on the spot movement to calm yourself earlier than your emotions go out of manipulate. Slowing your breathing is a

smooth and green approach to ease any worry or pressure you may be feeling.

An easy respiratory approach facilitates calm a panic assault:

Holding your once more as right away as you may, stand or take a seat down down effortlessly.

Place one hand in your belly and the alternative on your chest.

Slowly inhale through your nostril as you don't forget to 4.

Your hand on your stomach ought to upward push, while the hand in your chest have to slightly flow into in any respect.

Breathe in at the same time as counting to seven.

As you rely to 8, exhale through your lips, forcing as an entire lot air as you can out while furthermore tightening the muscle companies to your belly.

Chapter 9: Understanding Ptsd

Some threats someone has or may be visible can reason signs and symptoms and signs of placed up-stressful strain ailment. PTSD, known as (Post-stressful strain disorder) is a medical situation understood. As the call indicates, this occurs because of stress after a annoying occasion. The syndrome consisted of a cluster of signs and symptoms and symptoms and symptoms and symptoms, which incorporates hallucinations, flashes of trauma, advanced irritability, sensitivity to minor noise, sleep troubles, stopping any photo or reminiscence, which reminds the trauma affected character. If the ones symptoms do not coincide, the individual will now not have put up-traumatic pressure ailment. Such symptoms were common in humans who have skilled avenue injuries natural failures, which include earthquakes and hurricanes, fires, torture, physical and sexual violence, and conflict.

PTSD Treatment, Safe Alternatives

Big coins is crafted from dealing with PTSD. In the news, Post-Traumatic Stress Disorder has emerge as a advertising and marketing device for all scientific pills, whether or not or now not or not through offerings subsidized through the Federal Government or personal insurers. More importantly, this shape of PTSD analysis is based definitely totally on scientific remedy, no longer clinical technology or actual human understanding of our navy employees and girls and positive civilians suffered from. There are some corporations, for the maximum humanistic method to PTSD remedy, that concentrate on supporting human beings get via the worrying research and supporting people assemble a robust, rich lifestyles for themselves.

For instance, "Veterans find peace with equine treatment" modified into the mission of a contemporary-day channel ten news section in Sarasota, Florida, at the Circle V Ranch and rehabilitation center in Dade City. The venture of this ranch is to help veterans and number one responders with possibility remedy (Alternative to the use of pharmaceutical products). The farm offers with equine remedy to help the veteran and the pony, and through this carrier, the veteran will broaden inside the direction of his life. Another counselor at the middle states from the records that "they begin to reconnect with each exceptional as they interact with the horse. They will begin to speak with the community when they hook up with themselves; therefore, they may be able to begin reconnecting with their families." However, the ranch offers assist to the own family, for the cause that PTSD signs and symptoms impact all.

Therapy for highbrow health has become the number one approach to PTSD. The FDA warns of delusions, hallucinations, mania, paranoia, suicidal thoughts, homicidal ideas, violence, and plenty of more, which consist of psychiatric drugs. For a few, it involuntarily activates even as a person is exposed to the negative results of the medication. Staying in a psychiatric ward is a further stigma, financial burden, and each other danger to diagnose and cope with patients with medicines.

Dr. Gary G. Kohl has presently published a maximum applicable paper to the ones branded Psychotic PTSD, Bipolar, Depressed, Manic, and who in any other case have been spread out for prognosis, position on medicinal drug, and psychiatric remedy. A expert in worrying stress conditions, thoughts feature, non-pharmaceutical methods to highbrow health, neuro sender issues, meals additive neurotoxicity, and psychotropic drug issues.

This blessings sufferers who have had terrible drug reactions, advanced dependence, have withdrawal signs and symptoms and signs, and enjoy toxicity from the drugs themselves. In Dr. Kohl's positioned up, titled "Psychiatric Hospitals: On being nicely in 'insane areas,' if there are safety and insanity, how can we comprehend it? "This is a famous test posted in 1973 thru manner of D. L. Roshenan, which exposed the intense weaknesses of 8 psychiatric hospitals at that factor as professional human beings, like Roshenan itself, fake the symptom of being attentive to and admitted themselves to 12 separate psychiatric hospitals. 23 of the 41 sufferers were suspected via the usage of a medical doctor to be fraudulent, and ten have been accused of being each with the aid of the use of the usage of a psychologist and every exclusive body of employees member. "From this, 41 sufferers were as a end result rescued from being diagnosed with intellectual contamination and guarded in competition to the converting intellectual effects of psychiatric tablets. Therefore, requirements of health or folly once in a while can be wrong." Health and folly have cultural variations; for one society, what's anticipated can be seen as very aberrant in some different. One example is a well-known check with American and British psychiatrists and diagnostic discrepancies in each region. All researchers finished the equal interviews with a psychiatric employer of sufferers. American physicians loads greater often treated psychiatry than British psychiatry in this collection of cases.

"Psychiatric diagnoses even erroneously deliver private, criminal, and social stigmas which is probably now not viable to shake and which frequently closing for a life-time." Alternative remedies are to be had for all and sundry with PTSD symptoms or different highbrow health signs and signs, and clinical experts work to help you triumph over this issue. It guarantees more than it grow to be years in the past. The records is to be had right right here that will help you and your family get all of the records earlier than selecting your care. Some advocates can will will let you get right of entry to this facts greater correctly, as they'll be moreover committed to making sure the right to complete statistics.

What Are the Causes of PTSD?

To apprehend the entire principle of submit-annoying pressure sickness. This series of symptoms and symptoms grow to be first described inside the American Civil War 1860–1865. Physicians commenced noticing signs and signs and symptoms on each components of the warfare that stopped veterans from re-stepping into civilian existence. Some of the symptoms and signs and symptoms were excessive hallucinations, commonly associated with noises and conflict memories. Many veterans have suffered panic attacks that we now recall to be some factor that might cause conflict recollections, like a gunshot or a photo like a spray—and it would purpose PTSD. The signs of PTSD were extra considerably diagnosed over the years since the Civil War. During World War I, as an instance, it have become found that veterans getting back from War in a few unspecified time within the destiny of Europe appeared to be transformed in order that the humans on the the front door could not understand. This u.S.A. Modified into called shell wonder. By World War II, the military knew the origins of PTSD greater than well and started out out running on remedy techniques.

Nevertheless, located up-disturbing pressure sickness is not constrained to soldiers by myself. Anyone who has had an incident of a deep emotional wound in their lifestyles will enlarge PTSD symptoms. For example, a lady who has been raped may additionally revel in signs; if she is round peculiar guys or walks in a darkish hall, she may additionally have panic attacks, identical to in which her assault passed off. People who've skilled a top natural disaster may moreover have signs and symptoms of PTSD. Earthquake sufferers, for example, may be excessive fear if a few component shakes the arena, whether or not or now not it's miles truly as harmless as a street steamroller or an real earthquake. PTSD additionally may be due to vehicle accidents or a violent assault on someone else. Doctors showed that small children who underwent surgery had professional PTSD signs and symptoms and symptoms and signs and symptoms in the long run. Similarly, people with gunshot wounds may additionally moreover enjoy PTSD signs and symptoms.

It is likewise essential to examine that now not anyone with a incredible worrying event research PTSD signs. It is encouraging to recognize that there are new treatments available for those who have advanced signs and symptoms of PTSD that, in most instances, show remarkable consequences and permit the sufferer to head decrease again to the appearance of ordinary lifestyles. There is hope for those who be anxious through the sometimes worsening situation— life can once more be tremendous, and you may revel in normal.

Chapter 10: Symptoms Of Cptsd

The signs and symptoms and symptoms of PTSD are divided into four classes which can be utilized in figuring out a analysis:

• Re-experiencing/Reliving the occasion

• Avoidance behaviors

• Negative temper/thoughts/emotions

• Hyperarousal (feeling on aspect constantly)

We will now appearance similarly into each of these.

Symptoms of reliving an occasion encompass awful dreams, frightening mind, terrible recollections, or perhaps flashbacks. A flashback looks like you are going via that same terrible trauma once more. You relive what you believed was over and accomplished inside the beyond. You revel in the pain time and again, and also you can't forestall this from occurring. Imagine being significantly harmed as quickly as, however people with PTSD can also have that experience a couple of instances. The trauma truely maintains reoccurring of their minds and traumatizes the victim again and again, leaving the sufferer defenseless.

Avoidance can cause most essential upsets in someone's lifestyles. People with PTSD might also avoid all situations that remind them of the annoying experience. They may also elude situations that would "purpose" reactive symptoms. They also can moreover live some distance from the place in which the trouble came about. They can also additionally stay away from the shape of event that the trauma that occurred. They have been mentioned to keep away from acquainted situations because it brings again the terrible reminiscences of the revel in. They may additionally moreover moreover be afraid to move away their home and visit art work. They can also isolate themselves in an try and prevent themselves from being damage all another time. They can also moreover attempt to keep away from questioning, feeling, and speakme about the incident altogether.

People who experience trauma can also start to assume in any other case about themselves and people spherical them. They can also take a more aggressive approach to lifestyles. Their feelings, moods, and mind can also all undergo. They may also enjoy sensations of guilt, shame, and mistrust. They may also moreover moreover enjoy, or even accept as true with, that the whole global is evil and dangerous. They can also moreover feel numb and get bored in sports they used to revel in. Or they may "block out" the state of affairs altogether, like selective amnesia. They use this as an terrible manner to cope with their emotional ache.

Hyperarousal is even as someone is with out problem "startled." Their reactions are too immoderate for the given prevalence. They overreact to topics that do not require that form of reaction—for instance, leaping up on every occasion the cell smartphone rings. This is in response to the disaster. If you have were given been getting threatening calls within the past, you may sense on aspect and even scared each time the mobile phone earrings. You may additionally furthermore have hassle sleeping and might have outbursts of anger or even rage. Having hyperarousal signs also can make it not possible to do every day responsibilities like concentrating or simply taking care of your self.

PTSD may additionally co-rise up with extraordinary conditions which incorporates melancholy, anxiety, and addiction.

Causes and Risk Factors of PTSD

As I in reality have already defined, the motive of PTSD is a trauma that is not appropriately treated. This may be rape, torture, natural catastrophe, any form of violence, or a situation that brought about or must have caused bodily harm or dying to an character. Loved ones can also get PTSD after gaining knowledge of approximately the demanding occasion.

Anyone can get PTSD. Seven to 8 percent of people will experience PTSD sooner or later in their lifetime. Research has positioned that your genes can also furthermore have an effect on whether you're extra at risk of PTSD.

Risk factors may additionally moreover encompass experiencing past disturbing events, getting physical harm, being a part of a violent scenario, seeing each different character being harmed or killed, having a history of being abused as a little one, feeling helpless and hopeless, having no social guide network in area, managing any extra strain inside the aftermath of the trauma (rebuilding your lifestyles, recuperation, and getting lower back to regular) and having a information of other highbrow illnesses, or a substance abuse hassle.

It is vital to keep in mind that it isn't your fault to enlarge PTSD. You are in no way in fee. You are not prone-minded, and also you probable did nothing to deserve the trauma. You cannot flow decrease back and forestall the situation from ever taking vicinity. But you could, and you have to combat to get your life once more. You can take a look at new coping capabilities, and be given as proper with it or not, and you can turn this horrible and simply tragic revel in into some thing wonderful. Instead of seeing the bad, teach your thoughts to locate the immoderate fantastic. And sure, there may be a amazing in every state of affairs. You can be examined. You will falter. But please do no longer surrender. I have been thru it too. I apprehend. I without a doubt have empathy for you.

How to address PTSD

I will discover coping techniques that I truly have for my part used to help me and coping guidelines that I sincerely have placed effective that others have used. I advise you operate diverse them, no longer but one or . If possible, please do use they all to your recuperation from PTSD.

Admit that you have a problem. If you do no longer consider a trouble exists, you can experience you do no longer want an answer. By admitting that some issue is incorrect (or at least it can be), you could allow your self the freedom to are looking for out solutions. You may additionally even free up possibilities to get your lifestyles over again on the right song.

Educate your self. Reading up, mastering, looking films, and so on., will will let you advantage the essential know-how you may need on your recovery. It can also help you finish the stigma in the direction of humans with highbrow infection, which include your self. In addition, it will will will let you gather your sickness for what it's miles: an contamination. Knowledge is electricity, my friend!

Get involved via becoming a member of a guide institution, supporting a neighbor in need, doing a kind act for a person plenty less fortunate, or volunteering somewhere. This will allow you to experience related to the ones spherical you, assemble your social manual network, and see existence from a completely brilliant perspective.

Finding techniques that assist you lighten up is incredible inside the ones horrifying situations, which incorporates nightmares, flashbacks, and activities that trigger your signs and symptoms. There are many methods to loosen up, and a person need to use the ones which might be maximum useful to themselves, which incorporates, however no longer restricted to, deep respiratory, meditation, praying, aromatherapy, paying attention to calming track, taking a bubble bathtub, spending time with a doggy, or maybe assignment superb types of exercise which includes yoga.

You are distracting yourself. When triggering conditions upward push up, and you are not capable of cope with them at that moment as it need to be, it's miles essential to try to distract your self. You are giving yourself a damage with the useful resource of distracting yourself, it genuinely is good enough! Instead of wondering negatively, try wondering or doing some thing you want, like reading a e-book or turning up the music.

Accept the trauma for what it's miles and for what it's no longer. The situation you went through have end up highly scary, distressing, painful, or even torturous. But you have been robust enough to pull through it. You are a warrior! You had the strength required to conquer the situation. There is not any want to consider it to any volume similarly and live at the emotional ache. What accurate will that do? The trauma become now not your fault. It passed off. Things appear, and you aren't guilty. Please pick out out to permit it reinforce you and not wreck you! When your thoughts brings you again to this terrible, tragic memory, prevent it from taking manipulate of your feelings and feelings. You are on pinnacle of things, and you may no longer allow this adversity damage you.

Sleep properly. Since PTSD can reason lousy goals and nightmares associated with the worrying occasion, it's miles essential to undergo in mind the ones tips in case you are having problem together together along with your sleep. If a monster awakes you, do not forget that it is not occurring. It is simplest a terrible dream. Play a few relaxing tune and speak to a person till you fall back asleep. Also, attempt now not to oversleep and maintain on a ordinary sleep ordinary. If your nightmares preserve, you may need to peer a physician who can be able to prescribe a remedy designed for that.

Avoid illegal pills, tobacco, alcohol, and caffeine. These substances will most effective worsen your signs and symptoms and signs and symptoms and signs and symptoms and growth their depth and incidence. They can also moreover have an impact in your capability to sleep well. If you have got were given an dependancy trouble, I encourage you to are attempting to find remedy for that.

Maintain a high high-quality body of mind. Life has enough negatives in it each day. There is definitely no room to maintain on on your negative mind approximately past activities. Try letting circulate. Try cleansing your thoughts and ridding it of these awful mind. Replace them with wonderful matters together with every day affirmations, prayers, inspirational sayings, and motivational prices. Be awesome, and your mind will love you. Instead of seeing the horrible factor of the entirety, search for positivity in even the worst instances. Tell yourself it's going to all be actual sufficient. Have preference for a brighter and higher future. Allow your self to appearance the possibilities and doors as a way to be opened to you within the future. Let pass of the beyond and cling to the choice of what's going to be, not what changed into.

Keep the religion. In the worst of instances, we want to preserve the faith! Never lose faith in yourself, who you're, and who you need to turn out to be. You may be your private superb pal. You can be excellent for yourself. It is you which have endless possibilities for yourself. Never give up on your self. Also, if you maintain in thoughts in God, maintain in thoughts that He loves you and places you on this Earth for a cause. You should locate want that it's far He who has a improbable plan in your lifestyles. Things may go wrong, however it's miles all part of a bigger plan that we may additionally furthermore by no means be able to understand but must embody. Embracing this could allow you to discover peace internal your self.

Seek out a therapist, counselor, or psychologist. Preferably one that practices trauma-focused psychotherapy. Other treatment options used encompass cognitive-behavioral treatment (CBT) and Eye motion desensitization and reprocessing. A therapist will assist carry the pain to the floor. Once you can talk about it and vent all of your emotions, you can begin to heal the pain. You can discover ways to think in any other way approximately what happened. You will discover ways to take transport of it, allow it move, and drift ahead together with your existence. Ultimately, it's miles what it's far.

Find a health practitioner. You can appearance up medical doctors on the net or have your primary physician refer you to a psychiatrist. This form of physician will examine your case and decide if remedy could assist you to your recuperation approach. Certain antidepressants are idea to be very powerful in treating PTSD. The drug remedies artwork in your mind chemistry, which permits stabilize your thoughts, moods, and behaviors.

If you take a look at a majority of those recommendations, suggestions, and recommendations, you may be in your manner to a completely a fulfillment healing from your PTSD!

Chapter 11: Ptsd Symptoms Differential Diagnosis

A severe highbrow contamination that influences veterans and soldiers and lots of humans stricken by or witnessed abuse or violence is placed up-stressful pressure sickness (PTSD).

While the signs and signs and symptoms of PTSD may also seem much like the ones of numerous problems, there are big and massive versions. PTSD, for instance, may also appear to be anxiety-related signs and symptoms, which includes acute strain sickness, phobia, or obsessive-compulsive sickness. However, there may be commonly no stressful event to reason anxiety or worry in tension troubles. Or within the case of dread, this cause is not expert via most humans as a cause of situation.

The symptoms of acute strain disruption commonly rise up inside a month of a demanding incidence and forestall indoors a month. When signs and symptoms and signs and signs remaining longer than one month and comply with extraordinary sorts of PTSD, a person's prognosis can also additionally need to exchange from acute stress contamination to PTSD.

Although recurrent, repetitive mind are a symptom of each PTSD and obsessive-compulsive contamination (OCD), the idea-office work are one manner to parent these situations. With PTSD, the mind are always related to a worrying event in the beyond. Reviews in obsessive-compulsive disease generally do not relate to a worrying occasion in records.

PTSD symptoms also may be an adjustment illness due to the fact they are associated with anxiety following stressor publicity. The stressor is a traumatic situation for PTSD. The stressor must no longer be severe or beyond the "regular" human enjoy with adjustment infection.

The arousal and dissociative symptoms of panic sickness are usually no longer observed in PTSD. PTSD isn't a commonplace anxiety illness in that it's miles at once related to annoying events (it isn't in generalized anxiety infection) to avoidance, irritability, and anxiety.

Whereas someone who has PTSD can also be depressed, usually, PTSD signs and symptoms precede despair (in a person with placed up-worrying pressure sickness, it is able to assist provide an purpose for those depressing emotions).

In precis, someone's exposure to actual or drawing close demise, immoderate damage, or sexual assault with recurred intrusive signs and signs specially related to this annoying occasion can outline put up-worrying stress disorder. After the trauma takes area, a person constantly avoids stimuli associated with the trauma and research enormous mood and wondering modifications due to the trauma.

Anxiety Disorder Compared to PTSD

It may be difficult to decide the distinction amongst PTSD and different demanding pressure troubles. This capture 22 state of affairs is compounded due to the reality PTSD and different tension troubles, which consist of GAD, often rise up together. Learn how the two range, so you can learn the manner the recovery method begins.

Generalized Anxiety Disorder Signs and Diagnosis

Excessive fear and tension constitute GAD. Although most humans have a few issues or fears in their lives, a person with GAD is extra worried and demanding than it's far.

The following may additionally moreover seem to them:

• Relaxed or on the threshold

• Easy to experience fatigued

• Concentration troubles

• Faultlessness

• Tension of the muscle

• Disorders of the sleep sample

If you are going thru GAD signs and signs, do no longer combat it by myself. GAD differs from exceptional tension problems in that GAD signs must arise as a minimum six months earlier than a sickness is identified. "GAD affected 6.Eight million individual human beings, or 3.1 percent of the U.S. Population, in each given 12 months," the Anxiety and Depression Association of the united states shared 1.

Symptoms of Post-Traumatic Stress

PTSD is an anxiety illness that can boom traumatic occasions after an man or woman experience it. You might be involved, decided, or helpless. Symptoms of PTSD may also moreover additionally begin to intervene along side your day by day life. The following may additionally include those signs and signs and symptoms and symptoms and signs and symptoms:

- Disturbances of sleep pattern

- Faultlessness

- Outbreaks of anger

- Concentration trouble

- Oversight

- Felt sprung or scared

You may even maintain to relive the trauma. People with PTSD will revel in the subsequent trauma another time:

- Returns.

- Halluces.

- Dreams of nasty topics.

- Mental or physiological distress.

Those who have troubles with PTSD might also moreover try to avoid signs and symptoms and symptoms through using averting trauma-associated stimuli. These may be derived from highbrow pictures, thoughts, and sensations. Actual occasions, places, or devices can also cause them.

This prevention may be as follows:

• You or a cherished one do not need to speak, expect, or enjoy approximately trauma.

• You can prevent trauma-reminiscent places, sports, and individuals.

• You won't be capable of don't forget activities or a selected occasion.

• You ought to become bored in topics that you as soon as cared for.

• You can sense unconnected.

• You might also moreover furthermore feel or seem blunt to your emotion.

• You can find out it tough to check a really perfect destiny, a terrific lifestyles, or an ordinary life.

Symptoms of PTSD may additionally additionally moreover feel debilitating, however they do not need to keep your existence below manipulate. How to govern your PTSD can be located? Professional remedy, medicine, and speech treatment provide actual syndrome treatment, explains the National Institute of Mental Health.2

Discussing GAD and PTSD

Many signs overlap with GAD and PTSD. GAD is characterized, for instance, with the aid of large tension and concern. These also are troubles that could get up whilst someone struggles with PTSD. With every intellectual health query, human beings will save you locations, occasions, and those from being worried and involved.

In addition, there can be problems about mental fitness. Co-prevalence may additionally furthermore rise up due to the characteristics of 1 sickness because the chance elements for the opportunity. A character with GAD troubles and a traumatic incident can also revel in PTSD symptoms much more likely. This propensity to undue fear and misery can exacerbate a traumatic event.

The connection amongst PTSD and Headaches

Few speak of this, but there is cause to consider there can be common co-prevalence of submit-disturbing pressure contamination (PTSD). Although the attention of intellectual fitness specialists is a lot decrease than special PTSD issues, the relationship between PTSD and headaches is extensive. If you have got were given PTSD, you are more likely to boom diverse bodily conditions, which consist of diabetes, weight problems, coronary coronary heart ailment, and ache. For instance, 20-30% of human beings with PTSD stated issues with tension on the identical time because it came to grief specifically.

Patients with migraine or tension, headaches display extended exposure to annoying sports with regards to issues. Furthermore, approximately 17 percentage have PTSD diagnosed signs and symptoms and signs and symptoms.

Another have a look at discovered that 32 percent of OEF / OIF PTSD veterans say they have got headaches issues.

The PTSD / Headaches connection

Why human beings with PTSD may additionally moreover revel in troubles with complications isn't always absolutely clear. Therefore, strain have become associated with headaches, and PTSD symptoms and symptoms have to absolutely result in remarkably excessive pressures and emotional pressure. Moreover, headache patients will be inclined to enjoy extra stressful sports in their every day lives. PTSD can intrude appreciably with many elements and relationships of a person's existence. This probable creates more ache, which increases the chance of headaches.

OEF / OIF-veterans have immoderate prices of annoying mind injuries that account for the extensive style of OEF / OIF-veterans with PTSD said complications. In a few instances, someone with PTSD also can suffer from disturbing reminiscences that might growth the hazard of headaches. You may be more likely to enjoy headaches problems at the same time as, for instance, you were in an twist of fate or situation at the equal time as you had a head damage or a demanding thoughts harm.

Chapter 12: Strategies To Recovery

Creative Strategies

Tapping into your innovative facet may be an powerful manner of processing and overcoming a annoying experience's after-effects. Strategies together with artwork, song, and writing are feasible alternatives for trauma healing. These innovative alternatives can gain people who struggle with verbal expressions in their memories.

Art Therapy

The recovery blessings of artwork can come from many exclusive paperwork in numerous wonderful settings. This can be portray, drawing, coloring, quilting, or university without or with the direction of an art therapist, with a group, or alone. A researcher who interviewed a difficult and speedy of artwork therapists compiled a listing of the predicted blessings accompanying artwork as a recovery device, alongside facet decreases in hypervigilance, stimulated superb emotions and reduced tension.

As stated already, artwork permits for the nonverbal expression of trauma stories and recollections. It may be hard to get right of entry to the memory or discover the phrases to precise it, however art may be an effective outlet. Creating artwork may be a way to externalize the internal reminiscence and private it, which allows combine the enjoy as a reminiscence in preference to a current-day supply of distress.

Art can be a manner to slowly gain publicity to troubling stimuli associated with trauma (much like the titration approach). The use of art work is fun and reduces hypervigilance, whether or not or not the artwork is related to the trauma. This non-verbal approach is seen as lots less threatening and may make it less complicated to address the issues. Art remedy furthermore awakens emotion to stimulate emotional numbing, along side high-quality emotion. The approach of making can assist in stirring and experiencing splendid emotions. Art creation also can enhance a experience of control over your revolutionary space, enhancing self perception in expressing emotions.

One have a look at tested the consequences of coloring on anxiety. The authors located that corporations coloring an in depth format, together with a mandala, observed tension lower to a lower level than the preliminary diploma of pressure taken on the start of the take a look at. Interestingly, there was no decrease in tension for those coloring the loose-form of a clean piece of paper. It is notion that coloring on a layout, much like the one from a coloring e-book, enables set up the inner chaos feature of hysteria. There are numerous coloring books to be had in-store and on line, some complete of mandalas and a few especially for rest. Interestingly, this type of resourceful expression is frequently integrated in the Holotropic Breathwork stated in advance. At the prevent of treatment intervals concerning Holotropic Breathwork, customers will paint mandalas as a manner to explicit their studies. A have a look at of young adults with excessive ratings on a PTSD scale showed superior PTSD signs and symptoms after completing artwork remedy. There have been several art work modalities used on this have a have a look at, and the quality turn out to be growing a e-book of paintings that contains a picture narrative of every person's lifestyles story. Each e-book modified into made up of 13 collages or drawings and a hand-crafted e-book cowl. Other unique artwork sports activities that had been determined to reduce signs and symptoms of PTSD correctly encompass sewing pillows, beading jewelry, making ceramics, growing plaques, sewing leather-primarily based handbags and decorations for vacations or seasons. Supplies and thoughts for those artwork tasks and plenty of more may be placed at nearby crafting stores, and idea can be decided on-line.

Music

Music is used often in movies, television, or perhaps classified ads to persuade, sign, or alter our moods. Chances are you have were given got used track to mirror or enhance your contemporary mood or country of mind. Now era is demonstrating how music can alter mood and cope. Music treatment allows individuals who've survived trauma to relate to the healthful variations and create a strong and amusing environment. Music may be another deliver of grounding and make stressful reminiscences available for dialogue and processing. Like growing paintings, song can create a feel of control and unique the trauma. Music can allow human beings to connect with and precise emotions and connect with others, often through institution music remedy. Hypervigilance also can be addressed on this manner via the usage of encouraging tolerance of loud sounds or silence, similarly to a awareness through devoting hobby to music made through yourself or others.

One example is the use of loud drumming to specific anger or songs to lower tension. Specifically, tension-reducing songs are normally slow-paced and function a sincere rhythm. In greater advanced variations of tune remedy, thru the help of a music therapist, survivors can write and document track that creates an auditory narrative of the traumatic revel in or the lifestyles tale, much like the art work assignment said earlier.

A studies have a look at completed with a set of adults with PTSD that did now not reply to cognitive behavior treatment were given ten weeks of song remedy in which they were recommended to improvise music with loads of smooth to apply devices (like a tambourine) whilst accompanied via a track therapist presenting instrumental support. After the ten-week remedy duration, there has been a high-quality bargain in PTSD signs and symptoms. Interviews with the have a look at contributors located out that many felt they may get out their anger and frustrations through the tune they produced and afterward felt calm and managed.

Writing

The manner of writing can be a powerful tool for creativity and self-expression, similarly to putting phrases to and coping with trauma and brilliant excessive emotional critiques. Several advantages come from writing, including disconnecting a feeling of misery from the recollections of trauma, developing a feel of control and emotion regulation, and higher health and well-being. It is thought that the ones fitness blessings are visible due to the lower in inhibition via the disclosure of associated sports thru writing. Writing moreover creates the opportunity to make which means of the demanding occasion or include the occasion into present strategies of making which means that approximately the arena—in extraordinary phrases, to assist create a experience about your annoying event that suits your beliefs and fee structures. It is in particular useful to invite people to install writing down every day approximately their disturbing stories and the linked feelings.

In one check with university college students, members were asked to write down down for 20 minutes approximately the most traumatic and scary experience in their lives. After this writing length, the students stated that the occasion regarded more interior their manage and much less threatening than before the writing mission. They additionally located the occasion to be a good buy much less annoying in the present and not as vital to their lives. These are all very adaptive modifications in perception and impact tiers of distress. The university students additionally observed they had fewer intrusive thoughts and lots much less avoidance of the memory of the situation they wrote approximately. This pertains to a good buy less cognitive processing of the occasion, this means that that highbrow (belief) property are extra freed-up for one-of-a-kind excessive-order thinking.

Chapter 13: Dialectal Behavior Therapy

In brief, Dialectical behavior treatment or DBT is a form of behavioral therapy introduced thru Dr. Marsha Lineham, an American psychologist. She decided CBT as a treatment inefficient to assist people with suicidal inclinations. The basis of this treatment uses the fundamental ideas of the same vintage CBT however with extra variations to satisfy the best desires of humans experiencing excessive feelings. The number one intention of DBT is to empower you to manage hard feelings through sharing, recognizing, and accepting them. As you learn how to take and manipulate your feelings, you may higher recover from the damaging behaviors. DBT therapists make use of a balance of alternate and reputation strategies to build up this goal, that is missing in one of a kind treatment plans to address behavioral issues.

In DBT, therapists assist you locate the proper stability amongst acceptance and alternate through four without a doubt one in every of a kind elements:

- Skills training (in corporations)

- Individual remedy

- Telephonic education

- Consultation group of therapists

A normal direction of DBT includes homework and take-home assignments, which commonly keep for approximately a year. Many people can also find out it quite difficult to increase DBT skills in the starting because it consists of accepting your flaws even as running tough to trade them. However, with time, you could come to recognise that all your efforts had been worthwhile.

Summary

If you live with an tension sickness, you most likely renowned that feeling on top of things is a validating, valuable feeling. DBT assist you to reap this thru organization skills training, knowledgeable therapists, and competencies education. DBT is presently strolling on four considered one of a kind stages—

Mindfulness, Interpersonal Effectiveness, Distress Tolerance, and Emotional Regulation—to help humans get over their worst fears and depressive states. All the ones factors will artwork collectively to make certain that DBT gives you competencies that you can placed into exercise that will help you get complete manipulate over the way you revel in and live.

DBT Distress Tolerance and Mindfulness Skills

Now that the concept of DBT is apparent allow's circulate on to talk approximately the number one additives of DBT—Mindfulness and Distress Tolerance and their characteristic within the treatment of behavioral issues.

What are DBT Mindfulness Skills?

Mindfulness refers to taking note of what's happening inside the intervening time "on reason." When training mindfulness, you recognition at the prevailing experience, noticing something is taking location at the exact 2nd, not out of location inside the past, or questioning about the future.

Mindfulness is a few element opposite to being on automated pilot. While you are on automatic pilot, you're both doing matters out of dependancy or by using the use of way of rote. For example, many human beings relate to a circumstance wherein they arrive at art work but do no longer don't forget the automobile journey that took them there. That is due to the reality you probably did no longer need to reflect onconsideration on beginning the car door, sitting down, putting the crucial component inside the ignition, and many others. You simply did all this stuff automatically and discovered yourself at your place of job minutes later. Doing topics in an autopilot mode is not lousy. It is pretty useful in a way that permits maintain strength and time. Problems rise up even as you begin living maximum of your life on this mode as opposed to being gift in the 2nd.

Why Does Mindfulness Matter?

Mindfulness is sort of a magic problem that lets in you manage your sentiments and take a step back from excessive emotions. When you're taking a step once more and examine what's going on, you're lots less likely to enjoy out-of-control emotions.

"Mindfulness is powerful."

The blessings of mindfulness have been properly-researched, specifically throughout the previous couple of years. When you operate mindfulness to control your hobby, you open your self to a whole new global of choice. You do not need to behave and react out of worry, dependancy, or intense emotions. The everyday mindfulness workout has decreased distraction, improved emotional regulation, superior anger control, and decreased melancholy.

Mindfulness in DBT

Mindfulness bureaucracy the spine of DBT. It is the primary potential taught to the patients choosing DBT. It is not feasible to adjust prolonged-recognition appearing, wondering, and feeling patterns with out mindfulness.

"Mindfulness is the center ability underlying all one-of-a-kind capacity units in DBT."

It is vital to getting through hard conditions, resolving interpersonal conflicts, and regulating emotions. Mindfulness is also a primary element for gaining access to your Wise Mind, an important foundational idea in DBT. A Wise Mind synthesizes a Reasonable Mind and an Emotion Mind. Once you discover your Wise Mind, statistics what's herbal for you and appearing in step with it gets less complicated. The concept of mindfulness in DBT revolves round questions: "What to do" and "the manner to do it." These are referred to as the 'What' and 'How' abilties.

The 'What' Skills

Three abilties encompass the "What" of mindfulness:

• Observe

- Describe

- Participate

The Observe Skill

Observing technique noticing any direct sensory revel in. It is what you experience, see, flavor, enjoy, pay attention, and contact without judging it, labeling it, or reacting to it. This is difficult for maximum people before the entirety; your thoughts wants to label what is taking place round you as opposed to truely being with the sensations of an enjoy. While you exercise the Observe abilities, you allow your direct experience to take area with out looking to alternate it or pushing it away.

Like all of the abilties, searching competencies is experiential. This indicates that the highbrow know-how of this understanding isn't sufficient; you want to enjoy it for yourself to recognize it without a doubt. For instance, listening to the sounds spherical you, clearly noticing them with out passing any remarks, is an example of looking at the information of mindfulness in DBT.

The Describe Skill

The defined capabilities assemble on sensible skills. While gazing is most effective naked-bones interest—noticing a few aspect with out together with a label or a tale—describe includes putting the sensible experience into phrases, whether or not it's miles an emotion, idea, or a sensation.

It appears like a piece of cake, proper? Not quite.

Chapter 14: Ptsd And Relaxation

Generally speakme, a rest approach permits people lighten up through reducing their pain, tension, stress, or anger, for that reason making the maximum of despair, complications, excessive blood strain, and insomnia. In so doing, signs and conditions might also turn out to be more doable, however the trendy us of a of fitness also can moreover decorate.

Autogenic training, as an example, advanced with the beneficial useful resource of the German psychiatrist Johannes Heinrich Schultz around 1932, consists of short instructions lasting an average of 15 mins, which might be supposed to be repeated every day and that thru a series of visualizations motive at generating a experience of relaxation. Positions to workout Autogenic training may be freely decided on, despite the fact that locating one which can encourage the character to lighten up and attention on visualizations, together with lying down or sitting effects, is rather advocated. This method can alleviate pressure-associated issues due to stressful sports.

Christopher deCharms, a neuroscientist and social entrepreneur, founder, and CEO of Omneuron, a lifestyles era commercial enterprise organization whose generation is a pioneer in imaging strategies, together with Stanford University School of Medicine, has superior a live fMRI aiming at measuring and editing brain functions, with the final cause being the treatment of persistent ache. This method allows the affected person to control his misery with the useful useful resource of visually searching at his rtfMRI and checking his reactions in real-time. Then, through changing the latter, with the aid of ultimately blockading the pathways inflicting pain. Biofeedback, each different holistic technique, with the resource of manipulating physiological features through using unique devices checking "brainwaves, muscle tone, skin conductance, coronary coronary heart charge, and ache perception" (deCharms et al., 2005) also can play a function within the good deal of despair, tension and strain.

In simple English, this means that that with the aid of turning into aware about one's mind and perceptions on the identical time as pain is experienced, you can change that experience through switching to a brand new way of wondering and perceiving. In so doing, via way of taking manipulate over their mind and body, they're able to lessen or, through further education, even get rid of the possibility of experiencing that pain again. (deCharms, R. C. (2008). This artwork, which the National Institute of Health price range, seems to be a promising one for treating chronic pain, depression, and tension.

Biofeedback is some distance from a modern-day-day approach as it has been spherical for millennia in India and carried out via Yoga and Pranayama. While Yoga, it's miles a philosophical device based totally definitely totally on the workout of physical, intellectual, and non secular carrying events aiming at achieving entire manipulate over every the frame and the thoughts, focuses on a sequence of strategies and postures to perform this purpose, Pranayama, this means that 'prana' (existence pressure, breath) and 'ayāma' (to growth), is a yogic region which moreover originated in India and concentrates on respiratory bodily activities. The assumption of the latter is that for the reason that respiration is truly a need for the lifestyles of any residing being, mastering how to breathe successfully and profoundly can pretty enhance the health of the character via manner of the usage of strengthening the lifestyles pressure animating their frame.

Furthermore, respiratory is also seen as "the precept hyperlink amongst conscious and subconscious," which means that that respiration effectively is not amazing beneficial to our bodily however furthermore to our emotional and highbrow health. (Stanway, 1994, p. 286) Research has verified that Pranayāma may be useful in instances of pressure-related problems. However, it's miles strongly recommended to practice this form of breathing exercise beneath the supervision of a licensed practitioner to keep away from complications, injuries, and undesired facet effects. (Iyengar, 2011).

Yoga makes a speciality of keeping a thoughts-frame-spirit balance and correcting any imbalance earlier than harming the frame. Hatha Yoga is the type of Yoga in particular based totally on bodily physical video games, which embody stretching, respiratory, and relaxation. Yoga sees "the frame as a automobile, the thoughts as its motive strain and the soul because the Man's real identification" (Stenway, 1994, p. 284); consequently, it may be employed to "save you, treatment and manipulate quite a few issues (which include breathing, digestive, musculoskeletal and neurological ones)." It also can be an powerful technique to rehabilitate humans once they have lengthy long past thru surgical tactics and injuries, control disabilities, and cope with addictions. Yoga gets rid of strength (lifestyles strain, prana, chi, qi) blockage through the Asana or postures. Pranayāma, or respiratory carrying occasions, can help the frame detoxify just so the prana also can freely go with the go with the glide for the duration of it. It is meant to hold and restore homeostasis, the kingdom of stability favored for the body to attain maximum appropriate health. All body elements can benefit from the Asanas due to the truth muscle organizations are stretched and tuned up, the backbone and joints can keep their flexibility, and respiration and circulate can be superior. (p. 285)

Although rooted in historical Chinese philosophy and medicinal drug and moreover conceived as martial arts, Qi Gong and Tai Chi (the latter moreover referred to as Tai Chi Chuan) are holistic methodologies characterised by way of the usage of coordinated mild postures and moves, rhythmic respiration, and meditation and supposed as sorts of relaxation, preventive medication, and self-recuperation strategies.

The blessings of every strategies on health are many: They decorate the interest of the immune and lymphatic systems, the metabolism and tissue regeneration, and growth motion whilst lowering coronary heart price and blood strain. Oxygenation of the mind and all organs and tissues is likewise boosted, and a state of relaxation is produced with the aid of the use of decreasing the autonomic nerve-racking machine's sympathetic reaction (Trivieri & Anderson, 2002, p. 435).

The health advantages of every Qi Gong and Tai Chi have moreover been identified in our western international. Many for the time being are the hospitals and clinics that each endorse or have already protected them into their exercise. As for his or her application in cases of PTSD, those methodologies may be of terrific manual in handling ache, melancholy, and tension.

Chapter 15: What Is Psychotherapy?

Psychotherapy is, but, a conversation of a peculiar kind: that is, it's far both a hermeneutic and a dialectical alternate.

By hermeneutic, I recommend that therapists use interpretations of various kinds that set off customers to reconsider their positions. Such arrangements may also arise from the theoretical model wherein the therapist became initially knowledgeable. This is so; it's going to gain lower back to large discourses of various kinds—clinical, medical, restoration, sexual, cultural, social, and so forth. The technical device of a machine is, as I actually have defined, the tool through which interpretations are provided spontaneously in a healing communication (in 'closed conversations,' they will be brought with out preamble the usage of an 'professional voice').

However, interpretations can take a looser, favored form and are contained in anecdotes, analogies, allusions, and hints, to call only a few. These casual patterns have a extra profound importance. They element to the skilled therapist's facility in preserving special sorts of verbal exchange starting from the theoretical, technical fashion at one give up of the spectrum to the informal, ordinary fashion at the alternative. At the identical time, clients also can be using interpretations in their very personal to provide an explanation for their capture 22 state of affairs and interpret a few element therapists have to mention to them. This to-and-from interpretation and re-interpretation, now and again main to a synthesis of thoughts, is supposed with the resource of manner of dialogue. It is this that is, properly speakme, the cloth of psychotherapy.

However, the communicate we discover in treatment is of a unusual type: in particular, that it is attended to subjectively through way of using customers. Assuming that the therapist is heard to offer them sincere, applicable, intelligible, and insightful (Grice, 1989: 22-forty), the customer will are attempting to find to use the imparting to her non-public existence. That is to say; she may be able to no longer be involved with its purpose fact masses as whether or not it enables her to move on in a superb way (Wittgenstein, 1966: 40 four-45).

The texts with the useful resource of Wilhelm Reich and Arnold Lazarus pointed to the 'a few thing-goes' tremendous of recovery interpretations and remedy alternatives. Those identical interpretations and choices have been triggered with the aid of the use of the purchaser sitting earlier than them. I argued then that many experienced therapists, in exercise, do now not lease textbook techniques in treatment but as an possibility act as 'right chameleons,' the usage of all their arts of persuasion to hold clients spherical to a specific detail of view or to everyday their settlement to trying out a way on a trial-and-mistakes basis. In my assessment of some of restoration interviews, specially human beings with Gloria, I mounted that therapists who attempt too tough to impose a technique on clients regularly come undone due to the fact the conversational rules of recuperation conversations will generally go away the purchaser due to the fact the final arbiter on whether or not or not or not they may continue or now not. Although a minority of clients may blindly publish to indoctrination, the bulk (assuming they do not misunderstand what the therapist is trying to say) will respond on a spectrum beginning from enthusiastic reputation to outright rejection.

In the examples of recuperation conversations analyzed thus far, the formulations (interpretations) hired have once in a while been pragmatic (drawing interest to intentions and motives), on occasion theoretical (referring once more to mental theories), every now and then speculative, sometimes as an workout of authority, and sometimes as all 4. Other gadgets have moreover been used to pursue healing ends: metaphors, recollections, elements, script formulations, tag questions, and so forth. In move lower back, numerous responses have been elicited: indignant, humorous, ironic, resistant, beneficial, bored to death, at a loss for words, and many others. Occasionally the ones have added about new commands in communicate, but simply as often, they have got come to a conversational useless-forestall. But, inescapably, the cycle of interpretation-reaction-reinterpretation has concerned active voices continuously attempting to find to formulate the region from which the opposite is speaking. These continual uncertainties in interpretation make it difficult to research psychotherapy as a technique and very last consequences or as a proper approach.

Using Gadamer's art work on hermeneutics, I provide a model of psychotherapy that accepts the ones conversational uncertainties as a given. In so doing, I are looking for to resolve the questions raised from the start of this work concerning the relationship amongst concept and exercising and the uncertainties generated via the usage of a assessment between communicate about remedy to talk in therapy. Fundamentally Gadamer enables us understand why psychotherapy can not ever be a right technique (i.E., a technological information) and why accepting and statistics this leads us to understand how non-methodical (or semi-methodical) techniques can art work.

Chapter 16: What Is Talk Cure Therapy?

Nearly one hundred years inside the beyond, Sigmund Freud got here up with "the speaking treatment." Although he have become regarding psychoanalysis even as he to begin with uses the time, speakme approximately one's problems in a solid environment with trusted human beings has prolonged been tested to help remedy loss, trauma, and one-of-a-type emotional issues.

I now begin a talk of remedies for PTSD, starting first with a compare of traditional secular psychotherapies which can be now usually used to address this disease. Mental fitness professionals who offer the ones remedies normally have superior ranges are certified through the dominion, and acquire unique training to govern the particular shape of psychotherapy provided. You can be amazed that modern-day tips for the remedy of PTSD advise psychotherapy over medication and all super treatments. This is primarily based totally on a huge amount of studies displaying that the advantages of psychotherapy in PTSD an extended manner exceed the ones of drugs (and are without the side results that medicines have). Furthermore, the blessings of psychotherapy are greater prolonged-lasting than those on remedy, which may assist some mother and father best whilst the drug is being taken.

Many considered one of a type sorts of psychotherapies had been proposed for the treatment of PTSD. However, just a few of those were shown in medical studies (i.E., randomized scientific trials) to have the advantage. I will now speak each of these under and special reasonable intellectual strategies to treatment but have far a bargain a great deal less proof to beneficial useful resource their effectiveness. When discussing those diverse psychotherapies and intellectual treatments, I communicate over with an "impact period" (ES). The ES suggests the scale of the clinically giant effect that the treatment has. In certainly one of a kind terms, the ES is a quantitative degree of the advantages that you may get keep of after gift technique a path of the specific type of psychotherapy. ES's that suggest a small medical impact on decreasing PTSD signs and signs and signs and symptoms and signs and symptoms are the ones which may be -0.20 or toward 0; a mild product is characterised with the aid of the use of ES's within the shape of -zero.30 to -zero.60, and a tremendous clinical impact or gain is indicated thru ES's in the -0.Eighty or more bad concern. ES's additionally have what are known as "ninety 5% self assure intervals." This is a statistical term which means that 95% of folks that received the treatment fall inside the variety of values furnished. If a ninety 5% self guarantee c programming language includes 0, then the medical advantage of the treatment is considered to be similar to no remedy the least bit.

Most of the time, those research evaluate the psychotherapy being studied with a "manage" situation wherein participants get preserve of no remedy (controls is probably located at the waitlist to collect the therapy later or may get keep of "ordinary care," i.E., the care they may frequently get maintain of in the occasion that they've been not inside the take a look at). On occasion, the psychotherapy being studied is probably in evaluation with distinctive "lively" remedies (such as each other form of psychological treatment or medication). Of course, it is a lot more hard to reveal a big ES (indicating a clinically meaningful difference) if psychotherapy is in comparison to different treatments without a treatment or regular care. Now that can be more facts that you are interested in; it is able to be beneficial to study the consequences of psychotherapy with medicine and unique treatments.

Psychotherapies presently used to deal with PTSD can be divided into "trauma-targeted treatments" and "non-trauma-centered restoration strategies." I start with trauma-centered remedy options thinking about the truth that the ones are usually encouraged for humans with PTSD.

Chapter 17: What Is Cognitive Behavioral Therapy?

Cognitive Behavioral Therapy (CBT) is an technique that addresses dysfunctional behavioral emotions and highbrow strategies based completely mostly on a aggregate of middle behavioral thoughts and cognitive strategies. Problem-centered and movement-orientated approach practitioners use CBT to useful resource people cope with not unusual situations together with fear, pressure, and often extra complicated mental troubles.

Cognitive-behavioral treatment refers to numerous based psychotherapy techniques centering at the mind at the back of a patient's issues. CBT is likewise a maximum vital psychotherapy paradigm taught in graduate psychology programs. A survey of just about 2,three hundred psychologists in the U.S. Discovered that about 70 percentage makes use of CBT with distinct recovery methods to deal with melancholy and worry.

How Does Cognitive Therapy Work?

Cognitive-behavioral treatment is primarily based at the idea that human beings are specifically irrational and make many illogical mistakes whenever they verify the risks and blessings of their mind and actions from terrific conditions and guides. It can relate to out-of-balance emotions, collectively with rage and melancholy. But CBT is likewise used to cope with severa particular nuanced issues, along side publish-stressful pressure infection (PTSD), OCD, drug misuse, ADHD, consuming problems, bipolar sickness, and considered one of a kind ailments.

To gain success, cognitive-behavioral clinicians could have a sturdy interaction with their customers, which includes incredible listening abilties and an super individual healthy. This is because the affected person and therapist are strolling together to talk approximately the issues to hand and the motives for the affected man or woman's mind and movements towards those troubles. The give up purpose is to regulate thinking to feel a first-rate deal less constantly ugly intellectual situations.

The Global Coalition for Behavioral Wellbeing favors CBT. It has definitive research proof selling its utility in the restoration assessment of highbrow infection, gaining huge reputation among clinicians and sufferers alike. Increasing numbers of psychologists, psychiatrists, social human beings, and psychiatric nurses have become CBT schooling.

Research on CBT's effectiveness is powerful in opposition to a big sort of troubles. Those experiments are well-controlled, the data is efficiently reviewed, and the findings speak for themselves. Of starters, CBT has been demonstrated to have massive advantages at the equal time as managing bipolar despair, culminating in fewer treatment days, decreased suicide prices, and reduced tiers of parasuicidal or self-injurious conduct.

Precautions to be Taken in advance than Beginning Relational Cognitive Therapy

Psychiatrists, behavioral psychologists, social people, and unique intellectual fitness specialists undergo years of schooling and schooling, however with out this sturdy training enjoy, it's far feasible to exercise counseling. Before deciding on a CBT expert, one of a kind devices to examine encompass educational historic past and qualifications, together with any expert establishments to which they belong, inclusive of the Organization for Behavioral and Cognitive Therapies, in which most top practitioners are members. Review your data, schooling, credential, and license earlier than making your first appointment. The standard time period psychotherapist is regularly used. Make positive the therapist you choose out out meets the necessities of state certification and licensing for his or her specific assignment. The secret is finding a certified therapist who can in shape your wishes to the type and therapy. CBT is greater powerful in most conditions even as paired with numerous treatments, collectively with taking remedy. So, you could moreover want a psychiatrist to prescribe medicinal drugs besides your therapist.

The fee is one more aspect to undergo in mind. When you have fitness care, discover what's going to pay for all the treatment services it offers. Some fitness plans cover best a nice quantity of treatment classes a 12 months. Some might not additionally be included. So, make sure to barter the expenses and price plans with the psychiatrist earlier than the number one assembly.

Think approximately what problems you're experiencing that require care while you first assign. Although you need to even though paintings some of that out with your psychiatrist, a clearer statistics of your troubles will serve as a starting issue earlier. Do the research, and find a reliable Cognitive Behavioral Therapist. Check over again for their qualifications and experience, specially alongside aspect your questions. Some therapists won't meet the considered necessary qualifications. Don't surrender if you do no longer discover the proper one the number one time round.

Emotional Habits and CBT

It is usually stated that humans are creatures of dependancy.

Typically, this definition is used about our behavior—despite the fact that, in current years, we've got located that the manner we think is also not unusual. Since all of us recognize how we sense has a excellent deal to do with how we act, the low priced question is, what are my emotional conduct?

What Are the Emotional Habits?

Emotional conduct do have dimensions:

How we normally feel as we skip approximately the project of living our lives, each day.

If we react emotionally (again and again) to precise conditions/sports taking place in our lives.

Anxiety behaviors, despair, anger, irritability, helplessness, frustration, envy, worry, worry, and so forth. The mind and emotions can not be separated; they exist in unison for the duration of almost every second of existence. To be a person, in particular phrases, is to be in a country of non-forestall wondering and feeling—and the implicit complexities of that persevering with subjective revel in are in element every day. When we constantly feel apprehensive and involved about what others consider us, stressful about what our future holds, or angry and insecure about how our lives compete with others, it may be said that we've got got come to be used to repeating patterns. This isn't to condemn oneself or reduce the effect of actual-lifestyles sports and situations. The issue is to put us within the cause pressure's seat and propose that if we were used to those behavior, we're capable of re-accustom ourselves to them and one in every of a type / greater healthful traits.

Chapter 18: What Is Cognitive Processing Therapy?

Cognitive Processing Therapy (CPT) is a recovery technique that targets modifications in questioning which might be regular following a worrying event, along with changes within the manner you don't forget yourself and the area. The motive of CPT is that will help you learn how to have a look at your wondering and decide if there can be an possibility factor of view. Because of methods profoundly trauma changes your assessment, a part of this paintings calls as a way to flow yet again and revisit the stressful occasion to recognize how your contemporary—frequently unhelpful—belief procedures superior.

When we're uncovered to facts that doesn't healthy our view of the sector, we usually do surely considered one of matters in reaction: We each change the data to wholesome our beliefs ("perhaps I wasn't raped") or we trade our mind ("perhaps awful subjects do display as tons as suitable human beings").

Sometimes, perception adjustments grow to be severe, along side wondering I normally make errors or handiest awful topics display up (once in a while referred to as overgeneralization).

In CPT, step one is to combine the stressful experience into your notion structures and memories so that you begin to come to phrases with what happened. The next step is to regulate any overgeneralized ideals. Some of our emotions are biologically hardwired— like feeling fear in response to danger or unhappiness in reaction to loss—but lots of our feelings, together with guilt and disgrace, are idea to be "synthetic" because of defective wondering. The super facts is artificial emotions often dissipate following the modifications in wondering CPT enables cultivate.

Cognitive responsibilities, which include some thing as smooth as labeling gadgets, set off the logical part of our brains, similar to the prefrontal cortex, which allows adjust the emotional elements of the brain similar to the amygdala. Using your words to talk approximately and examine the demanding occasion calms overactive emotional responses. The purpose of CPT's healing sporting activities, which we'll explore under, is to increase flexibility on your wondering and guide your capability to think significantly approximately what you've been announcing to yourself about why the disturbing occasion came about and what it approach approximately yourself, others, and the arena around you. "Stuck factors" are terrible trauma-related thoughts or beliefs which might be exaggerated or distorted in some manner to be able to in the long run obstruct your recovery. Specifically, stuck elements are the elaborate techniques you evaluate the worrying event, just like the not unusual perception that during case you'd acted in any other case, you can have stored it from taking location. These beliefs might be new (placed up-trauma), or the trauma may likely have served as confirmation of some poor mind you already held. For instance, a person who, earlier than a disturbing occasion, located exceptional be given as actual with in authority figures much like the police may additionally furthermore start to increase a contemporary belief that police are nugatory and untrustworthy due to the truth they weren't able to reply short sufficient to save you an assault. In evaluation, a person who went through a comparable situation but already had trouble trusting authority might verify their prolonged-status ideals following the trauma.

If you've been questioning the same subjects over and over yet again ever for the purpose that your disturbing occasion, without reconsidering those mind or exploring opportunity thoughts, the critiques have likely become routine and entrenched on your ideals. To start to shift those idea patterns, you must approach your mind and critiques with an open thoughts and a willingness to task your assumptions.

CPT have become evolved to cope with quite a number problems and highbrow health problems, which incorporates PTSD, depression, tension, man or woman issues, troubles with substance use, and troubles surrounding self-esteem and self-idea. CPT has been carefully researched, and there is strong evidence for its effectiveness throughout severa populations. Study outcomes recommend that individuals have visible extraordinary decreases in self-said PTSD and other trauma-related intellectual fitness issues inside the direction of remedy and 6-month comply with-ups.